This & That

Whickwithy

This & That

All rights reserved

ISBN: 978-1-7348221-5-1

This & That by Whickwithy

First Edition End of 2022

Previous efforts:
Sentience
A Sentient Perspective
Beauty & Fiction
Millennium
Book 6
The Sentient Struggle For Transformation

Infini Entendre
   (Infini Entendre is poetry, very little of it applies
directly to the grand scheme of our humanity, but all
of it applies indirectly)

   If you desire to read further, after this book, I
would suggest skipping *Beauty & Fiction* and *Book 6*.
They seem redundant.   *The Sentient Struggle For
Transformation* is paramount. You should read one of
them *before* reading this book.

The following is a format that I previously used in chapters of a number of books. In this case, it is the book. Each is an insight, independent of the preceding and following insights. They are only connected by their *attempt* to see clearly. In this book? No promises. I am not human yet. That would take another lifetime. Many of the insights follow the thread of our humanity. This time, I separated them by lines of dash-marks.

This book has hardly been edited. I just don't have the heart any more. I have written seven books explaining what the hell is wrong with humanity and you still don't get it. I know many have read the books. Maybe the shock is just too much to absorb in short order. That is the best I can hope. The worst thought is that the dim-witted animal will never get what I am saying. That the prehuman is content to remain prehuman.

If something doesn't make sense at all, then it was probably a mistype. If it is convoluted, well, I am not trying to explain anything in this book, really. I'm just making observations.

The sad state of prehumanity, especially since I now can see our humanity vividly, is enough to bring anyone to the brink of despair. No, I don't despair. Thank goodness for my rhoetry. Otherwise, I'd be done.

I guarantee you there will be cryptic remarks in which it will be almost impossible to understand their context.

This and that

or, **Blow by blow**

We are not living a sentient reality. We continue to live an animal's reality.

Imagine the blind leading the blind for more than three millennia. Imagine an animal on which sentience slowly dawns that never gets the big picture. That is humanity up until this point in time.

We have never had a clue what it means to be sentient until now. Even now, it is only a single thread thrown out in hopes that prehumanity doesn't drown it its own muck.

We have accepted only half of our sentient state. Intelligence. The more crucial piece awaits. Until we accept our sentience in full, we will remain a demented animal.

We keep trying to fix the small stuff (i.e. everything but humanity itself), never realizing it is all small stuff until humanity becomes human. It makes it, as Shakespeare so eloquently stated, a tale told by an idiot, full of sound and fury, signifying nothing.

We have swallowed hook, line, and sinker the idea that we can't ever change significantly. It is the nose-to-the-grindstone approach of an animal. Pick away at the small stuff, as if it mattered at all, and never take a close look at what is wrong with humanity.

Read *The Sentient Struggle For Transformation*

I won't put a link. You will find that in my profile. The book is available on just about any bookstore's website.

What do you have to lose by considering that we remain an animal demented by its sentience *for no good reason?* That we are a demented race is obvious. If you can't see that, don't bother reading any further.

Once we accept our sentience, everything changes. We become a loving, sentient, human race. No god is going to get us there.

It only remains a tale told by an idiot because we have not achieved our humanity. It is easily done.

Our human characteristics await us.

We are not just an animal. So far, we have concluded that we are an animal with heightened intelligence. That just makes us a demented animal.

There is far more to sentience than we have ever imagined. It has to do with awareness. We are far more than an animal, or can be, once we accept our sentient state.

I've mentioned and praised *Kama Sutra* in many of the previous books. While it was a bust, at least it concentrated on where the problem lies: coitus.

Not some alternative to coitus because we couldn't ever make it work the way that a sentient race expects.

A tale told by an idiot

We have accepted the tale told by an idiot as if it were cast in stone. It is not.

What is humanity's worst enemy? Humanity.

Who wreaks havoc on our planet? Humanity.

The universe, all told, is a rather benign place for a fully sentient race. There is nothing left to fear on Earth for a sentient race *that fulfills its sentience* (yes, and asteroid could smash us to smithereens or the sun could go nova. yes, that is, for the moment, beyond our capabilities. Do you think our internecine nonsense helps us overcome those obstacles?).

There is a reason we have been running around like lunatics for more than three millennia. It doesn't need to remain that way. We have been living a lie.

I have explained, in detail, how humanity finally attains its state of sentience, its humanity in less that one hundred years or three generations.

No more deceit, delusions, or disruption. No more acting like a dim-witted animal. No more traits of the animal. No more witless violence.

The qualities that humanity has always sought but never attained *for more than three thousand years* can be ours in relatively short order. Honor, integrity, dignity, self-respect, in other words human behaviour, can be ours.

I have to say, I never expected it to be this hard to convey to humanity that they can be human and, more importantly, that they are not yet.

In actuality, it never crossed my mind. I never thought of how to convey the most crucial insight since the beginning of time. I was way too caught up in ironing out the details, which took twelve and forty years to grasp.

I won't get into the details of all of those years. I've written that elsewhere.

Men are cheesy. How hard can it be to grasp that statement? Men put on all of these acts of being human but they are not - yet. Since the beginning, men have known something has been missing and all they ever did was run for cover - and remained an animal. They accepted the animal's premise without using their intellect to discover the reality of sentience. There lies the one and only problem impeding our humanity. We remain tightly coupled to the animal for a single reason.

Out of all of the things that humans expect out of life, men are missing the only one that heals the heart and makes a human. It's as easy as that. We have not looked into this subject because it horrified the animal.

Imprint this on your brain, animals are dimwitted. We are not. Because it horrifies the animal in its witless state, we have looked no further and, thereby, remained an animal.

All we ever had to do was accept that we are human. The new phrase to replace the worn out statement, "we're only human" that has echoed down the millennia is, "Omigosh, we are human!" We are not bound by the same rules as an animal.

Even though it is rare at this point in time, because of the menagerie of nonsense we have accepted from the animal for three millennia, we can, believe it or not, think. More importantly, we can think with the heart. Even men.

That makes all the difference in the world. Men can easily think themselves out of the trap in which they have been caught since the first man quailed at the big bad world. Actually, I've already done all of the thinking. You just need to accept reality. It's time to put the animal away, permanently and decisively.

Please read, *The Sentient Struggle For Transformation.*

We can become a human, sentient, emotionally-balanced, rational, stable species. We are not yet. Three generations is all it will take, maybe even less. Once it starts, it should snowball quickly.

I realized just today another step in my progress towards understanding.

There was the initial study of religions, cultures, institutions, and the like, that took forty or so years. And, there was, of course, the twelve years that I've mentioned often, after the initial study, in which, lightning struck. I spent the last twelve years straightening that all out in my head, so that I could explain it in an acceptable way.

But, the key, the absolutely essential ingredient, was the six years that preceded the lightning which I spent exploring life through the lens of rhoetry.

That was the first six years of my rhoetry. It was an intense period of rhoetry creation. Not really with anything in mind, other than humanity has been seriously messed up. That was always in the background, never in the forefront. It was just ticking away in my mind at some deep level. What the hell is the matter with humanity??!?

That absolutely led to the state of mind that led to the lightning. I call it attempting to see around corners or looking left while gazing right.

The more I study the effect, I think it is like sneaking up on your subconscious. I know it sounds crazy but I am truly beginning to wonder if the subconscious is not suitable for sentient beings.

It is where animals stash all of the trash with which they cannot cope. It is no more than an animal's coping mechanism. We should have overcome it long ago. But, there is one subject that continues to drive us crazy because it has *never* been allowed out in the open. That is disastrous beyond belief.

The subconscious is where all of the nonsense comes. We have been failing to cope with something that only applies to animals. We are not just animals. We can think.

The nonsense we accept locks the animal's purview into place. The subconscious kinda sucks.

My fondest poems, though, the ones that really blow me away are the poems I wrote for the last six years.

The timing is a bit complicated. Altogether, it was eighteen years of intense poetry. Six preceding the lightning, twelve more accompanying the effort to break the lightning down to its elementary components.

In the last six years, the poems that are fondest to my heart were written. You may see a very few of those (it was over five hundred, for sure, maybe six hundred to date). Mostly, I hold those close to my heart, in the absence of their muse.

Make love *to* you. Think about it.

Let me try, again. A person is not human until the realize that making love it a *two-way* affair.

Surprising to me, this is just as true of *both* genders. They remain an animal until that revelation.

We have never ever questioned the failure of coitus. Even now, with all of our openness about sex, we dance around the question. The reason is we have fatally accepted the failure of the animal.

Once, we succeed at realizing the the failure that almost all animals endure, does not need to be a *human* failure. We think or, at least, we are equipped to do so.

==========

Let me say, here, that this book is not about how we become human. That is what the previous seven books have been all about.

It is just that new ways to try to get it through your thick head that we are not human yet keep popping up. I am hoping that, if you have not read *The Sentient Struggle For Transformation* yet, you will.

It's kinda important.

My latest annoyance. I was pondering, once again, two questions I would like to put to an AI. Then, I thought about how Musky owns ChatBot or whatever it's called. I decided I could do without.

That led me to the point that they were attempting to gather info on the users, just like instagram. You must give them a mobile phone number.

The thing is, when you ask a bot questions, some monster animal disguised as a human could easily attempt to understand you better, push your buttons to influence your behaviour. For the maniacal animal, it is all about manipulating humanity or, I should say, prehumanity.

I have no doubt that, once we become a human, sentient, emotionally-balanced, rational, stable species, that won't matter for the many reasons I explain.

For now, I'll just pass the questions on to you. Now, there's a very good idea, if everybody swapped the questions with others to put to AI, would that confuse any attempts at manipulation? Would the unintended target of AI manipulation just be repelled? It seems likely.

Anyways, here are the questions:

1. Can you write an Operating System that would allow me to do what I desired on a computer? The language may need to be more precise but I would sure like an answer.

    You are free to ask this one, if you please.

2. What is the matter with humanity and how do we fix it? In this case, nobody else could ask this question in the way I desired. I think I could lead an AI to the answer. It might even be revealing in many ways. I'm always seeking answers. That question, above all, haunted me for a lifetime. It no longer does. It's sad to think that I might get it across to an AI but I have had such a hard time getting across to prehumans.

I don't expect anyone to ask this question until they are firmly human. You'd never be able to lead an AI to the correct answer, otherwise.

Okay, it might be interesting to see what gibberish develops if you are still only a demented animal. Not really. That is all around us today. We keep fixing the small stuff.

I was just writing some poems and, as usual, a breakthrough came.

Those lifetimes of achieving transcendence and, all the while, damning myself for not lasting long enough to share it with the one I love.

It took lifetimes to learn that lesson. It took lifetimes to overcome the foolish shame.

I will admit that I am incredibly smart but that, also, was due to circumstances. There's nothing special about me. In the earlier part of life, I was fine-tuned, due to circumstances, to live inside my head.

I was influenced by an unlikely set of circumstances to shut my mouth rather permanently (I know, right?). It led me to particularly keep my mouth shut when faced with words portraying the prehuman stupour. In that way, because of the circumstances of never opening my mouth regarding the stupour, I never got caught up in it.

What else was a boy to do except think? I was going to add "like mad" but thought that would be pejorative and misleading.

Later in life, as the reality of what is holding us back hit me, I *had* to concentrate at an intense level.

I had a small section in the last book in which I described my worries about people getting confused. Particularly women. Since I am not one, in such a situation as I describe it, I'm at a loss as to what makes them skeptical about it. I know for a fact that many have read each one of my books.

I thought of another worry that applies to most everyone (I can't think of an exception. Is there a fear that life without challenges would be boring? Of course it would be. There will remain challenges galore. Just a lot less pain.

Let me give a ridiculously simple example but it goes to the point.

I have had a broken big toe for a very long time. As it froze in place with age, I had to spend all of my time and a great deal of my thought on moving in such a way that it would free up the big toe. It was painful but that's not the point. The pain was only part of what I needed to concentrate on in order to make my walk more natural and less painful.

What I realize, with this *unnecessary* pain, I was missing out on exploring the sense of feeling the walk. I know that sounds lame but I also think it is one of those characteristics that we lose from childhood.

We forget to sense the amazement all around us. That is nothing but a damned shame. I'm all for informed innocence but I would really like to shed the armour that I have had to wear for so very long. It's another *unnecessary* burden that we have not yet shed.

It is appalling the aspects of childhood that we deem discardable.

=================

I am so right about what I suggest in *The Sentient Struggle For Transformation*.

Until all of humanity has principles and can distinguish reality from delusion, we will remain lost.

I think I know where we may be headed if we finally become human. For one, we would quit breeding like rabbit, start being human, and have some thought in our heads besides getting our rocks off.

That can't happen until we become human about sex. Then, everything changes.

I think, under those conditions, along with the certainty that we will no longer need humans to fill the 'jobs'. I put jobs in quotes because a human doesn't need some 'job' to go to in order to feel needed. Humans have a natural talent for wanting to do things. If we become rational, then those things we want to do become rational, also.

Anyways, at that point, it seems to me that we could set up a system that *housed and fed everybody*. Beyond that, it would be up to the individual to decide exactly what they wanted to do with their lives. Without the impediment of nonsense to blur the image, most people are going to want to contribute. In fact, I would guess there would be less people sitting around *wanting to* do nothing than ever before in history.

What will be interesting is to see humans do without the need to find shelter and food? People are naturally invested in their lives and life, in general. It's what we do!

If the old broken ways no longer concepts of the animal become exposed and discarded, the universe is open.

Okay, a little more than food and shelter. Education and the internet would be helpful. I wonder if they aren't one and the same - in a truly human society, where the internet is not full of nonsense. Do you know that one of the biggest industries is porn? There is no need for porn when everyone is feeling good about their ability to love. The whole idea of perversity gets turned on its head, finally.

I can remember some scifi books (even Star Trek, for that matter) that got into the action-packed life of a prehuman. Subtly, posing the question, what happens when all the bad guys go away?

Can you really doubt it would be a good thing? It can't be bad that there isn't a threat behind every corner any longer. Do you think there is some kind of toll on life?

That's called old age and death. There's the only toll that counts. Hopefully, you've already read my thoughts on that. Death doesn't really count if you take the role of reincarnation seriously. It doesn't matter whether it exists, since you don't have to bother with it in this life. It just keeps your feet beneath you. If nothing else, it gets one to think about the lives of those that will live long after they are gone. That, also, is a good thing.

I once read a theory that the expansion of LGBTQ was nature's way of reining in the insane population explosion of humanity. It also should rein in the male rage.

Not a bad theory and it would probably work to some extent. To rein in the male rage, though, by making them human seems a lot more reasonable to me.

I am intrigued to have found another answer. The baffling behaviours of men have remained a puzzle to some extent, even though I have known the answer to what drives me crazy of more than a dozen year.

What drives them crazy is utterly obvious to me now. But, *why* do they react the way they do remained a bit baffling.

All of those rich guys that are putting on their bizarre act in order to get a attention...

Sometimes I wish I had titled the previous book, *The Sentient Struggle To Attain Transformation*
It's just so long!

I think humanity will discover its by-necessity methodical pace, once we become human. There is one exception to that, I think. Fusion energy. It will free up humanity and begin to end the damage caused by fossil fuels.

Of course, that is only possible if we catch on to human life quickly enough.

We need to hit a point where we begin to plan our future rather than just jumping off willy-nilly at anything that can make a profit.

I admit that could be a long way down the road that we start being so human.

First, before we can reach that level of beauty, each of us will need to be so confident in humanity that we finally rely on ourselves.

This is the other side of the studies I did in institutional structure and religions. If everyone is stable, then there are no shysters. No one is out for themselves over the needs of humanity as a whole.

If you ask me, this is what will end up being the most distinguishing feature, next to loving coitus, between a real, live, dyed-in-the-wool human and an animal. To put it in words, animals are out for themselves. Humans are out for their species (I would have used 'race', but you can see why I wouldn't, I think.

Whenever I publish this, you can be fairly certain it will be because I feel death approaching. I can see now that I will be able to write forever on this subject.

I have to laugh as I finally realize it. Of course, the biggest change in the animal branch of life since the first act of sex billions of years ago is going to have a lot to reveal! Duh.

Well, the only other possible reason I would publish this is if the lady I have adored might be willing to read this. Long story.

The real point of this, though, is that, once again, I am going to excuse myself from editing services.

This has been hard enough on my over the last fifteen years. I think, by overcoming a massive resistance to change (my resistance, not yours (i.e. I hate prose), I have honed my skills as an author. So, there should not be too many seriously damaging errors in typing or stream of thought.

There will probably be a lot of hanging 'dashes', though. Sometimes I just exhaust my brain before I am finished with a thought. You might very well find a stray at-sign or hashtag, also.

Once we are human, we will also be able to self-regulate our population. That is big. Once that happens, humanity will become self-sufficient. I don't want to explain all of the detail behind that. You'll just have to take my word for it.

If *The Sentient Struggle* doesn't convince people I can think, then this won't matter. No one will read this ever. If they did, they wouldn't get it anyways.

Another lesson in all of this that I have had to learn is that Nature ain't perfect. I mention this for a lot of reasons but the one on my mind it ticks. I would hope that the same would be true of other monsters, like mosquitoes. Unfortunately, I've heard good enough argument of the necessity of mosquitoes to give me pause on that one.

As I mention somewhere above, we will learn to be methodical. We have the capability, just not the sense, to pursue efforts like this. In other words, today, it would be done from an obsessive profit motive.

I don't know how we will organize as humans but one thing is certain. There might or might not be a profit motive but it won't be obsessive once we become human.

It's getting weird. It's like there are two of me. The one that has to contend and communicate with prehumans and the me that is trying to attain his humanity. The more the latter comes into effect, the more difficult it becomes to return to the former.

I am convinced that any man that makes a reasonable effort can become physically loving in the form of coitus.

The scientific evidence is that the glands in the crotch cause the beginnings of ejaculation and orgasm - for both genders. The rest? I have only proven to myself. Now, I admit, I am incredibly unusual but no special powers.

All I really did was never ever accept the bullshit that we call home. That led to everything else. Including the most difficult capability to attain loving coitus. Control of the muscles in the crotch.

I learned early that those *types* of muscles can be controlled. When I was young, my sister loved to tickle me cruelly under the arms. I learned to control the reaction of the muscles on the torso under the arms because of this.

Extrapolating the experience to control the muscles in the crotch was straightforward (I believe women need to learn the exact opposite, so to speak), once I realized what was going on. It was the latter that took forever. Because of the delusions we have accepted.

I am not a superman in that I learned it. It all started with just never accepting the bullshit. The difficult part, the part that took a lifetime was to replace all of that bullshit with something that made sense.

The actual muscle control was infinitely easier. The rest of the techniques I noted are just dead easy. The control of the muscles in the crotch is something that any human male should be able to learn to do.

Old Age, Part II
I can't get over it. This whole old age thing was really getting me down for the longest while, but no longer.

I have been overcoming the most distressing injury that has plagued me for ages. I absolutely love to walk. I had a big toe that was essentially frozen in place. That, in turn, due to the funny walking, affected other parts of the musculoskeletal structure. Between that and the damaged back, the pain was relentless.

Now, just as I'm getting to the point of despair, the toe breaks loose enough to walk normally. I cannot describe what a relief it is. I was really getting worried about other creaking parts.

I know. It's still getting older. I guess this substory within a scifi book, Ringworld (mind-blowing speculation all around), about these beings called Pak Protectors always inspired me. Keep in mind that this scifi was just full of alien beings.

It ends up that the Pak Protectors were old humans that had juggernauted into another stage of life. It's pretty amusing really. He suggests that the hardened bones, etc made for a superiour physical being and the age gave the potential for superiour experience and thinking ability.

I kinda agree. As has been seen over the last decade or so, age alone certainly doesn't assure thinking ability. Even so, it does allow for the potential of a thinking being that is well experienced in the effort.

I have to return to one of the main topics that I *attempted* to discuss in *Millennium*

I've often mentioned that we should be human within one hundred years from the time we begin to take achieving our sanity seriously.

By beginning, I mean that the concept that loving coitus is broken goes viral. It becomes commonly known.

That is far different from living within a human environment. One hundred years from our start date, we should be prepared to assess the prehuman situation. In other words, at that time, we should be able to sort out fairly well what needs to be adjusted and what messes are just the result of prehumans running the show.

More and more, I am betting that the bulk of our problems will have little to do with any of the structures or endeavors that we pursue (other than the accoutrements of war and violence) are unsound.

It is that there is a prehuman at the helm of every single effort (including these books). Some may will their way to acting more human than some others but, all it all, their prehuman.

There is the 90% of the brain that is confused about what is really going on. There is the foment below the surface (yes, I think it is that common).

Anyways, don't think that one hundred years will make human existence a picnic. But, we should be, at least, packing the picnic basket.

I have tried to explain this (to myself) for quite a long time. I will never be fully human in this life. I have way too much baggage that continues to sink me into the prehuman delusions.

So much mysticism that skews the picture. The belief in luck. The coincidences that I still put down to Serendipity as if it were a mystical force. The latter, I can't even fight too hard. It will take lifetimes before the human race is able to discern what is real and what is bullshit.

Let me stress this. It should be at the beginning, really, but so should so much else. This is not about you. It is not about me. It is about the human race.

Do you see why I bring it up at this point? We have never worked as a race. Until we become human and accept our sentience in full, we never will.

One of the 'signposts' (I mention 'signposts to the future of a humanity that works' in one of the books) is probably exactly that. When we work together as a well-oiled machine will be a significant signpost that we are attaining our sanity, emotional balance, and sentience in full.

It is very frustrating actually. It is like having glasses on that show me what humanity can be (especially as I feel it growing in myself) and, then, have to deal with all of the distortions of the prehuman. Social media? Forget it. Can't stand it.

All of the media mania that people use to have a social exchange, the blaring, blazing split of humanity into its fractured state is on full display. How am I supposed to deal with that? It saddens me to think of all of those that do.

In real life, like going to a store or something. That's fine. It is when the delusions become prominent that I get utterly disgusted.

I have to reiterate something that I wrote in one of the earlier books (I haven't a clue which). The change will be amazing to observe. I so wish I could be around but that's not likely.

It will be only a change in tone, so to speak. I become more and more convinced of this. The interactions won't change (other than war and violence). The topics of conversation should change radically as time progresses. It's just the awful incomplete feeling that threads through every conversation will be gone.

I shrug off the gloom of not seeing some sign that you idiots can move on. You are all so caught up in "what's happening" that you never look to see what is *really* going on. But, it comes back. I think I can cope if I stay in my Blue Bottle in every way. Well, but that's a long story.

Anyways, even if I keep going, I'll be gone before you guys get a serious clue. This is a tricky part. I have to expose myself to some of the nonsense some of the time in order to see if anyone is getting a clue.

Altogether, I see some slight chance that I am getting through. Or, at least, that the ideas that I have been hammering away at for a dozen years are getting through. Whether it is due to me ... who knows?

I believe, as with anything new, it's day has come. The signs seem to be everywhere. The biggest signs, though, are that we are seriously breaking apart as a race. Not that we are attaining our humanity. Just that it is time. Even so, if anyone reads the book(s) through and grasped what I am saying, whether they can accept it or not, the avalanche has begun.

Like I said, I see hints that people are, finally, after three thousand years, tired of playing the games.

That is another part that drives me crazy and has done so all of my life. I would never play the games. They were stupid. Sorry, no other word for it. They were a confusing mire of nonsense regarding what should be obvious. Why all the games?

Well, that was the first forty years. The last dozen has been pinning all of the puzzle pieces in place.

At least I was distracted from the game of nonsense. Mostly. ;~j I found the most fascinating example of the puzzle. She drove me on.

I was just pondering another aspect of our prehuman existence. The absolutely non-functional way in which we progress is awful. It's shows in everything we do.

It shows in how we cope with stupidity, which we often mistake for 'evil'. We are still functioning like a disjointed bunch of animals that don't know what they want in life, other than a good meal, shelter and, foolishly, fame.

It's worse that that, though. Our prehuman progress is a stumbling, fumbling effort driven more by personal grandiose than any desire to move humanity forward.

Maybe the biggest lesson we refuse to learn is that a methodical approach to progress would outstrip the bumbling, desperate manner in which we wreck every aspect of our world.

The only world in the universe in which we can hope to thrive and survive. That may seem counter to some claims that you have rattling around in your head. What about Mars? What about all of those planets that will be discovered at some point in the future (probably near future)?

It is a matter of prospects. How quickly can we utterly destroy our existence on Earth versus how quickly we can establish a independently viable footprint on another planet? That means that enclosed environments are no longer required. Just remember, it has already been fifty years since we first stepped onto the Moon!

We have been racing to the finish line for so long that we have learned to rely on winning the race.

Why do you think that humanity remains demented? Make no mistake, as long a a large portion of humanity remains demented, the whole race remains demented.

Do you think it is education that will finally grant us our humanity? If so, you have a poor opinion of humanity.

Do you think ridding us of all of the demented individuals will change everything? I am sorry to say, they would crop up, again.

No, there is something fundamental that is missing. Yeah, still trying to get through to you.

It is truly amazing that humanity has not been able to attain its humanity because, for more than three millennia, we have avoided the single incongruity that forces us to remain a demented animal.

We act as if it is no big deal that men are lousy at coitus. The ramifications of which are seen everywhere. It, of course, creates a demented background for humanity and the male, in particular.

I must not be remiss: Spoiler alert: men have never needed to accept the failure of the loving event that coitus should be. We have only hamstrung ourselves by avoiding facing the situation squarely.

Of late, we have hemmed an hawed about it, while *still* never addressing the situation. Mostly, though, we *still* dance around the subject like it doesn't exist. We *still* are willing to break our backs rather than face the stark situation that never ever needed to exist for a human sentient race and, yet, has brought us to our knees.

Of course men can learn to last as long as the woman desires. They are human. Unlike an animal, we think. Animals are driven only by instinct. Humans can overcome the inept, destructive instincts of an animal. I mean, Duh!!

We continue to carry the disastrous misconstruction that there is an necessary upper limit as to how long a man can last. That is true of a stupid animal. It is not true of a human being.

It has destroyed our sentient existence for as long as we have been aware of it. *That* has been a very long time. That is the thing about sentience. While we have tried, we cannot make our awareness go away, short of a lobotomy.

You probably never even got this far into this insight. If you did, you probably don't understand the ramifications of men remaining failures at something so central to liberating the loving nature of humanity, a tentatively sentient race. Read the book for both the clarity and the way in which men become fully human.

Let's see if I can provide an analogy that works. Imagine a den full o lions. Are the others affected when one goes mad? What happens if nearly half of the lions become demented to some degree?

What continues to astonish me is that we keep acting like the ones that are unsatisfied with our state, our lack of humanity, our awful prehuman state, are crazy.

Let's be clear. It is the (pre)human condition that is utterly insane. The ones that realize this are considered insane. The accepted practice of all of humanity is to dumb people down, drown them so deeply in drugs, that they no longer care.

That is considered the cure for the insane (pre)human condition. Riiiiight.

All of our existence is based on a single lie. We have refused to admit the utter failure of humanity to attain its humanity. It is attainable. We can be human rather than a demented animal. Right now. Not at some distant, vague future date. But, right now.

WABOFI

There is an element of the animal sexual situation that makes me wonder. It is another example of how we have distorted our image in our desire to distort reality in order to hide our foolish shame. Female animals don't seem all that thrilled about having sex. In our utter confusion, we have rationalized that it makes the male or the race better in some way. It is an excuse for the male's relentless pursuit of sex in the face of the faulty sexual practice of the male's inability to make it fulfilling for the female.

There's no advantage to humanity of having a male gender that fucks up the most extraordinary interaction of existence. That is for animals.

The interesting, outlier that I cannot answer, is whether women will *still* not want coitus very often. I would mention the other forms of sex but the key point is whether women getting their rocks off will *still* be less attractive than it is to the male.

Personally, I don't believe it for a moment but that doesn't prove a thing.

In essence, it doesn't really matter. Once men can quit hiding from their own shadows, once we all quit lying to ourselves, we will know for certain and be able to deal with it.

I am not concerned about men wanting orgasms and, thereby sex, more often than women. Once we are not hiding anything about sex, once men can accept that they can provide a loving experience, the whole picture changes. We can deal with it, once we quit acting like the lack of coital orgasm for the women doesn't shake our very foundations.

This one insight is worth the whole book. This is one that I have also been struggling with for a very long time. It truly has been like a chess game or a puzzle. Just because I can pin down one piece does not mean that there weren't plenty of other pieces that still didn't fit quite right, or needed to be move along, if you will.

I still don't know how to explain it well. I can only hope that someone that reads this book and begins to comprehend what I had to go through can explain it better. Probably not.

It also plays on the idea of lifetime relationships. We are not just animals. Animals have to rely on each other for survival. Humans need to rely on each other for far more. We need to be able to operate as a race, not just as a bunch of individuals. I could probably write a book on that insight alone. That one statement may define our problems better than any other.

Our inability to operate as a single entity all goes down to our inability to accept our sentient state in full. All due to our inability to accept a single incongruity of the drastic change from being just an animal. No, we are not 'just human'. We only remain that way because we act like individuals without the common interest of all of humanity because we are lying to each other about a single subject. Forget lying about it. We don't even mention it. It is like the supernova in the room that burns everyone of us until men can finally figure out that they can last. Then, we can quit ignoring the whole fiasco and move on into our sentience.

The universe is indifferent. It is not bad or good. Yes, the whole human race could get hammered by some random event. But, I think overall is the case is that any planet on which a sentient race develops, probably has astronomically good odds of having the leeway to find their way. To put it another way, an sentient race that does not find its way is the more likely destructive event that ends that race. Probably before they can expand off of their own planet in any serious manner. So, if that is true, that pegs the necessity of our advancement into our sentient state pretty much immediately. One of the factors that I have pondered is that, for instance, much closer into the center of our galaxy and life itself doesn't have much chance of surviving millions of years. One supernova or another will be close enough to assure that no sentient race ever has the time to evolve.

'Nature' is indifferent but it seems to have intent. The real question for me is where does 'the universe' end and Nature begin? In other words, is Nature the intent of the universe? You'll have to read my other books (*Millennium*? maybe?) to get the rest of that thought. I term it the trajectory of Nature (versus the trajectory of life (though closely coupled) or the trajectory of sentience (or humanity).

Animals are indifferent and have no intent other than to continue to exist (true existentialism. *remember* we are no animal!). Humans are different. We can distinguish good from bad, even though we have ignored, in embarrassment and without any answers (until now), the worst trait of the prehuman condition that cannot coexist with sentience or, at least, sane sentience. I don't know why but Nature is set on a trajectory. So, it seems obvious that the intent of the universe *is* the same as the intent of Nature.

Nature's intent, somehow, is to create a race that could distinguish bad from good or, maybe a better way to say it is that humanity can distinguish between acceptable and unacceptable. We can't even begin to fulfill that until we acknowledge what is unacceptable about coitus.

More than that, it has created a race of beings that can seek out the good in the universe and nurture it. It's just that the very special race of beings doesn't know it yet.

I want to take a moment to describe the evolution of the beast. I have tried and tried to make this clear, to bring to light the way in which we have compounded the original deceit of our humanity over the ages. It may have been the most difficult aspect of all of this to convey. It is not obvious. I talk of the proliferation of lies due to a single lie.

We are becoming so distrustful of humanity that many of us no longer even try to make a commitment for a lifetime. We are certain of betrayal. To me, that describes the ongoing accumulation of lies, of disappointment with prehumanity, and acceptance of the beast better than anything.

We initially, thousands of years ago, had a sense of sentience. It has been disappointed repeatedly, when it comes to love, noble characteristics, and any human (as opposed to prehuman) motive. We have learned to grub along as an animal would.

It is this that breaks my heart repeatedly and continuously. My own absolute faith in humanity is hurt severely every time I see someone give up that celebration, that revel in sentient existence.

My 'faith' is not the blind faith in some imaginary god. It is a faith in *humanity*'s potential built on the very clear little acts of loving, caring, and kindness that go on every day all around us but are overshadowed by the bizarre interactions 'at a distance'.

That inability to span the gap of distance shows exactly how broken humanity is. The difference between me and the rest of prehumanity is that I do not accept our demented paranoid state as our final resting place.

I want to explore this from another perspective. A perspective that brushes up so close to the central issue of our insanity.

The growing distrust of everything (pre)human is the most appalling result. It is a matter of everyone looking around and seeing the awful mess that the *pre*human creates. The difficulty lies in the belief that we are already human. We are not.

Everyone chooses their particular flavour of insanity in order to point their finger at "what is really wrong". Shades of the split personality. We accept half answers. Am I the only one that can see that both sides have a point? Am I the only one that can accept that they are all only half answers? That neither has a sentient answer to our dilemma?

It has been going on since the beginning but it is getting far worse, and it is accelerating. We niggled away our sentience.

The way I see it is that, in the very distant past, everything was looking up. Our sentience was new and it was a joyous experience. We built out from nothing into an amazing existence.

Even as we were building out from the magnificent gift of intelligence, attempting to explore this amazing new development of sentience, distrust was already sown.

Our sentient awareness was aware but it had already been beaten back into the subconscious (a realm exclusive to the animal, I believe. in other words, once we become human, I am not so sure the *sub*conscious will exist). The appalling, bewildering answer we have concocted is, "we're only human".

We are not human yet. There lies the real problem.

We made all of the appropriate gestures, appearing to take an open, even-handed examination towards *all* aspects of existence. *Seemingly* thinking cogently, exploring deeply, and investigating *all* important aspects in detail. Even then, it was all a sham. Or, to state it more forgivingly, it was real enough, except for that one uncomfortable subject glaringly missing from all investigations. We just wouldn't discuss it. We still don't.

Maybe it was as I've often said. The subject was not new. What was there to learn? Sex had existed for a billion years. We believed that we were fated to be lousy at coitus so why bring it up? Even though our sentient awareness knew better.

It was also, at this point, that the pompous authoritarian attitude that is global in nature appeared. It came into being as we avoided what it was really all about. Rather than answers, we accepted pompous proclamations of no import. Our sentient awareness was subjugated. The rest is history.

Even then, sex, *always* in particular coitus, was the outlier. We turned out the lights. Just rut in the dark. Let's never notice the monster we created, the elephant in the bed.

Unless, of course, you were conquering some 'other' culture. Then, it was rape and pillage, *just like an animal*. We really haven't changed that much at all. The animal remains and lurks.

The perverse insanities that pervade sex says it all.

The raping and pillaging happens within one's own culture, one's own home, often enough. There is just no getting away from it until we eliminate its source. The missing self-respect.

Our animal legacy had gotten the better of us from the very beginning. Coitus was such a revel (for the male at least) such a transcendent experience, that they wouldn't let it enter their heads (or anyone else's) that something was missing.

Men ruled. Fuck everybody else. Of course, it didn't develop that way. That's just the way it worked out. More exactly, men and women were just doing what animals had always done. At some point, long ago, it began to dawn that there could be, should be, more. At that point, we were at a loss. Men and women had to justify the awkward situation that did not suit a sentient race. Considering our limited state of development, it is no surprise that we came up with some really stupid resolutions, gods, and broken ways in which to move forward.

In some ways, it seems game theory has been working, wearing away at the animal since the beginning. It seems part of the trajectory of life. Game theory seems a fundamental aspect of animate existence. Win-win is better. The dumb animal never had a clue. Brute existence does not suit sentience or win-win.

This last insight seems at the very core of sentience. There will be no love, in its fullest expression, until a win-win situation exists. It is like existence itself insists on an intimate sentient relationship that is built on a foundation of physical love, which leads to equality, and equitable circumstances allowing sentience to flourish. Humanity, then, can move forward into its humanity. Or, continue to waste away its existence as an animal until it destroys itself thoroughly and irreversibly.

This is a nit-picky point but, after seven books, yeah, I'm getting nit-picky. I'm guessing most people would think it is awesome to write books. I'm not enamoured. It's more like being trapped. I don't think I've used this phrase throughout the books.

AAaaaaarrrrrrrrggggggggggggggghhhhhhh!

Believe me, I would much rather be writing rhoetry. I think I've said enough in prose after this book. Goodness, I hope so.

Maybe I can begin to write my insights in rhoetry. That should work fine since they will be so far beyond the scope of humanity for a generation or two.

By then, maybe folks will take to rhoetry and its power and be able to understand the nuances

=====================

I've been pondering the whole mating ritual. How much of it is due to the animal and how much is due to a more basic aspect of nature.

I was thinking about 'dress-up'. Whether it is man or woman, everybody plays dress up. The specific dress up I was considering, though, was women's.

All of the make up, the desperate desire to stay looking young. Is that human or animal?

The idea seems to be that it is to attract the most promising mate. There are two aspects to inspect. The most promising mate and what is used for attraction and the interaction between the two.

The interaction has to do with what the man desires. If he only desire sex, then all of the attraction is directed towards looking sexy. In that case, looks that portray young, vibrant, and ready to get laid is a good call.

This really is *another* level to the ongoing investigation of the last dozen years. What happens when the man is driven by more than just sex? We see a diluted version of it today.

The more I think about it, the more I am convinced that we will be able to seek someone with whom we are compatible with a much clearer eye than ever before.

Once we become human, the mating dance will be about compatibility far more than other qualities that the animal and our distorted concepts of importance find attractive.

For some, it becomes a substitute badge for male virility in the absence of loving coitus, to have a trophy wife. Men seek some way to disprove what they feel is true: they feel like lousy humans. Most of mankind's manias are due to that fact.

The reason even our best efforts today remain diluted is because the man has no confidence in himself to attract a mate. He often relies on the animal version of attraction.

Strong, which gets subdivided with humans into physical strength, wealth, power, delusions of grandeur, etc., is the drive because men just want to get laid and prove they can. They know they are no good in the sex department, so they attempt to make up for it by taking "strong" to lunatic extremes.

Regarding a human future, we would be attempting to study a man that knows he is as good as any other man at coitus *and* knows that every other man is just as good as he is at sex.

He certainly will not be overcome by some woman wagging their tail. Sex will, of course, remain an attractant but, when all things are equal on the sexual front, things change. This is going to take some thinking to take it further. I think the simplest answer is equality and equitable circumstances rather than the confusing blur that we have experienced.

I even get a glimpse of that confusing blur, like a high-speed snapshot of it all. I'd rather spend time, though, on investigating the future state of love, when it actually exists in its human form.

In the future, men will still want sex. There is an unknown wildcard for me, though I think I know the answer. How much women want sex when it works right for them?

Women seem to be able to take sex or leave it without too much trouble. They are not physically (rather than physiologically), driven to sex. The near absolute need for men to relieve the sexual pressure buildup as the sex glands fill still makes it paramount for a man to find release.

Now, I have two wild cards. How much will women desire sex when it works for them? And, how much will men still be driven *just by sex* once they know that can succeed at loving a woman? I guess that adds another joker. How big a deal is 'sexual compatibility' once everyone is achieving orgasm?

I think the last one answered a lot of the previous wildcards. I feel certain that sexual compatibility is a much bigger deal when men don't know what the hell they are doing.

So, sex becomes less of a pressing matter if it works and something *more* can be attain.

In strides love. New wildcards are dealt.

I've finally convinced myself beyond doubt that men can conquer their urges that cause them to fail at coitus. As I stated the question to myself, I realized it was a trick question. The answer is in the question. Of course men an conquer themselves. There are so many reasons to be certain that men can succeed at loving coitus. *Every* man.

I was just thinking of another element that has something to say on the subject. Until men conquer themselves, they will have a desire to conquer women. That's a trick statement. The reason men want to conquer women is *because* they know they should be able to conquer themselves and, yet, haven't.

Nature would not leave such a gaping hole that could not be filled by a human, sentient race. The whole physiognomy of it makes it clear. We were made to be able to consciously control any muscle. It is similar to dancing. The only reason some people don't know how to dance is because they have been too frightened to try.

Think of men as a gender wide stage fright. We never talk about it. We only indulge in it in the dark.

Men's minds freeze up after failing (due only to inexperience) a few times. They think they've tried everything but they never knew what to try.

Now, everyone does. In fact, another thought hit me today regarding the subject of men's success.

Everything I have explained must become common knowledge that anyone can rattle off in an instant.

Because it is not open and common knowledge, men freeze up. They never learn what to do because no one has really ever set their minds to the problem. Everyone has just skirted the issue. If anything, there is consensus that no better than a few minutes should be expected. We should be ashamed of ourselves for thinking so. Instead, we remain ashamed of the results.

Jump around and measure just how long men last and *use that as a yardstick??!?!* Or, even worse, which I'm pretty sure is the case in some cases, *they just ask the man how long he lasts.* That tells you just how far anyone has looked. "It's all a mystery."

No wonder everyone loves murder mysteries. It makes everyone feel at home.

But, I keep digressing.

Keep in mind that it is not a matter of relaxing the crotch muscles completely. It is a matter of not allowing them to twinge, flex, or relax. Just hold them steady. That is another reason for the exercises. The muscles in the crotch get very little exercise in your daily rounds. They get clamped down to end an outflow from the body or twinge their minds out during sex. That's it. Of course, they need some exercise. Remember, it's only about two minutes of your day.

I am more and more thinking that the act of love will become a really awesome experience once we sink our teeth into it (so to speak) because it finally works to all expectations.

It truly amazes me how people get caught up in minutia. Sometimes it amazes me that I didn't put a bullet in my brain a very long time ago.

I can see way too many views and understand each of them so thoroughly now. It's kinda funny. Now that I have completely transcended the idiocy (okay, maybe not *completely*), I can almost understand all of those neanderthal views. I guess it is because I can now distinguish between the human and the animal. So, it is much easier for me to accept the awful views of people like Murdock, Koch, Trump, Biden, Musty now that I can realize they are all nothing more than prehuman animals with the wit of a post. All of them putting on an act. Love the double entendre.

I am beginning to suspect the reason for the subconscious' existence is for subjugating our sentient, human, loving state to the millions of years of the animal's state of being. That is, a state of bafflement, state of stupour. The animal is very comfortable in its stupour. More than happy to remain witless.

Maybe it is actually a case of the subconscious *being* the state of the common animal. It is almost like the ability to communicate verbally lit the fire of our sentience, making all of existence more substantial. *Except for the ones that we leave stuck in the subconscious, like coitus.* Before it was all of sex, since they were one and the same in most cases, but, now, it is exclusively coitus. That's fucked up.

The subconscious is the result of repressed sentient, human, loving thoughts that don't fit in with the remnants of the animal. It is like they are trying to break out of their imprisonment in the subconscious.

The more I study what lurks in the subconscious (and not just the awful stuff), the more I think it will be a profound adaptation. It reminds me a lot of my suggestion concerning the other 90% of our brain. It has to do with sentient innocence. An enhanced innocence that sees things as they really are and can deal with them as a sentient, emotionally-stable, balanced race of beings.

I guess I have to think that animals see things as they are, also, but, because they are only animals, they can't even attempt to do anything about it. There lies the difference.

Like I have stated before, the phrase 'perception is reality' is a warning, not an observation. It is saying the stupour is okay.

- This dash, in particular, is tentative but I will leave it.

While I am uncomfortable with the following statement, I will leave it. It just sounds too pompous and round about for me.

It has *always* been that men had to take the lead by following in the woman's footsteps to their humanity (which we have not done). Because we (men) had so much to learn, we will become the teachers before it is over. We have to learn it from the ground up. That makes for good teachers. Men will finally have earned their role as leaders.

I really think there is something here. It is just that I cannot yet articulate it well. There are too many unknowns at this time to really articulate what I am trying to say. Again, like a chess game. Too many moves ahead.

So far, men have led in order to deceive. Call it a penance.

I don't know that I want to get into this further but I can't hardly leave it hanging like that.

Men have been a failure (sorry, I just can't take the effort today to try to be other than blunt today). What women can take for granted, it has taken men three thousand years to get to the point that they have even the possibility to grasp. That is profound, by the way.

As such, they will know it thoroughly. As I write this, because of the renewal of the species every one hundred years or so, I am not sure this is true. One hundred years or so from the point that we step off the platform onto the train of our sentience, all will be equal (in soooo many ways).

If the deeper understanding doesn't come to the fore in that one hundred years, it may never happen. It is in that transition from prehuman to human that so much will be available for rumination. After that, I really believe men's proficiency at coitus and love will become second nature.

Then, the prehuman becomes nothing more than history. Read Santayana's quote on history.

Maybe that's okay. Maybe that natural acceptance is what it is all about. I am just big on understanding. Truly understanding.

Also, men will go through the process of learning, to some extent, as they approach and pass puberty. Maybe there is some important learnings in the minimal effort it will become.

It does give me some encouragement that what I am doing in writing this book may be worthwhile.

Did I make the suggestion that men will become the teachers sound like a pompous male trumpeting? It is not meant to be so.

Maybe what I said earlier covers the case. Women and men moving forward, hand in hand, will connect all of the remaining dots. That makes more sense. A combined effort, finally.

A lot of our past seems to make more sense with this thought in mind. Not that our past makes the slightest bit of sense but, maybe a better way to describe it, is that this makes it clearer.

To me, it explains why some men have striven so hard to explain what is going on. The male gender, overall, doesn't understand a thing, yet. So, a few, at least, have always really been trying to be honest and explain it for themselves.

Dreams. Once we become human, what happens to dreams and sleep? This has been creeping out of the caverns of my mind. When I talk about ending our nightmares, I am not sure I am just talking figuratively. At least, I am considering the necessity of nightmares for a prehuman. I have to believe they no longer need exist.

I am becoming convinced that our nightmares are due, in large part, to the inconsistency of our existence. Our sentient awareness screams to be released from our subconscious.

It makes me think that, maybe, all of our dreaming is trying to sort through the nonsense of the previous day and put it in context, try to fit it into what we know is true and should be the case for our existence. It is no surprise that, with all of the nonsense that we accept, nightmares are the result.

Since 90% of the brain is left contending with an awful state of confusion, delusion, and denial, it comes out as nightmares. It is our caged sentient awareness attempting to make sense of nonsense. Maybe that is why I had so few nightmares. I lived the animal's rendition of human life as little as possible.

That makes me think that, maybe, dreaming - as crazy as it sounds, maybe even sleep - is a remnant of not being fully in line with our sentient potential. In other words, our minds will not have any debris to sort through, once we become human. If so, the ramifications are far greater than the apparent ones.

Of late, I have been engaging online with a number of women that are haunted by nightmares. It is really disturbing. Not surprising, I guess, at all. Woman's situation sucks. I don't think there is any other solution than attaining our humanity and providing equality and equitable and loving treatment for women. Before it's over, the equitable treatment of all humans.

I hope it is clear that this is what I have been driving at all along. I can't say, though, that I ever stated it clearly. We treat each other like dirt. Not just women. We treat humanity, as a whole, like dirt. We treat our Earth like, errr, trash. We treat all of existence like dirt. We revel in hate often enough.

I just keep thinking about these things that perplex me. They seem like crazy things to consider but, if I hadn't considered a *lot* of crazy things, I never would have uncovered the source of our troubles.

These are things like 'signs' and what I call, 'serendipity'. It is really nice to just say it is all just hocus-pocus or, in other words, coincidence or, worse yet, *intentional* coincidence.

Let me start with the last because is weighs on me. Right when I needed it, I ran across someone that knocked me loose. It has always seemed mysteriously appropriate but did I, so to speak, force the situation? Did I adore her just because I needed someone to prop me up?

I am not the right one to ask but, still, even after long, long, long consideration on every aspect, I don't think so. She is just flat-out special and only someone that was flat-out special could have joined me on the journey. That it didn't work out that way was my own inept way of handling it. No need to go there. If you can't figure out by now why that was true, there is not point in explaining.

I'll mention one in particular. My awful prose.

I have been exploring the idea that our sentient state completely revolves around coitus. In other words, that our sentience is dependent on that act of coitus. It is truly fascinating. If only we had trusted Nature.

First and foremost, Nature lit our brains beyond that of an ordinary animal. What could have caused the phenomenal development of the brain? What could have stirred the human to wonder? Nature made it so that we gaze into each other's eyes during the transformative act of coitus (even though we usually turn out the lights today). I just have to wonder if it lit our brains beyond that of an animal. Eye to eye coitus is truly a wonder.

I realize how outrageous this sounds but, if you can think about it for a minute, it makes all the sense in the world. No other animal, but one, looks into the eyes of their mate during the most transformative act of existence. It seems very possible that this forced our brains to kick into a higher gear. During the act that stirs the nerve endings throughout the body like nothing else, the brain stirred from its witless quiescent state into a higher gear while gazing into one's lover's eyes just seems to make sense. I can just see the male brain beginning to peer past the veil to take into account the horror that the experience is not shared.

It is really neither here nor there, just an interesting sidelight. But this is. Because we turned the lights out, we went mad. We couldn't face the failure.

I don't want to digress too much at this point but I have been wondering about emotions. It is another area that I think needs to be explored that has mostly been taken for granted or ignored or *analyzed* into its grave. To quote wikipedia, there is currently no scientific consensus on a definition. My own thoughts are that it is not a matter of science that is important. It is a matter of the heart. Anyways...

Coitus was initially accepted as it was. As questions regarding coitus began to be asked or contemplated, they were suppressed with a vengeance. Examples are everywhere.

I have to say that getting high on pot or cigarettes are really good for a disturbed prehuman. I just wonder if they will have the same attraction for a stable, emotionally-balanced human? I don't think so. As far as I am concerned, drugs, liquor, etc are all just escapism from a situation that is so mixed up that everyone is looking for some stability, even fiction. Sentience should be fun for all, sooner or later. Why would anyone want to escape, if so.

I'm really beginning to love this writing. At least at this time, I feel very good about my explanation of the problem in *Transformation*. So, I can delve into other subjects, finally and, like has happened so often in the past, I have been equipped for it by life.

I have stumbled my way through life. I am a slow thinker but an incredibly thorough thinker. So, by the time I figured out what mess I had gotten myself into, I was ready to cope with it.

Like I said, stumbling through life. I've always been fond of the idea of serendipity. It was like some supernatural being that helped guide the way. As I think of it now, I wonder if it isn't anything other than a willingness to see things through with a side helping of utter honesty.

I have to think that a lot of people have wondered about me. I learned early, from a lunatic dad, that the only way to deal with lunacy is not respond to it. Any other reaction just digs the hole deeper.

I can still recall most of the real showstoppers in detail. It's just something about certain statements that just catch my attention and I log it. When they are that weird, I just don't respond. It must put a lot of people off. I just sort of stare at them. Just like I did with my dad.

A certain girl has been a mystery to me for so long. I finally get what it is about her that just blows me away. She re-invents herself regularly.

You have no idea what a huge relief that is.

I'm not sure how to explain. There are a million different little things. But, piecing them together into a whole gives a pretty clear picture of what is going on. For me, she has this mercurial nature that I could never understand.

She reinvents herself. That just makes her especially fascinating for me. It is the reason she reinvents herself that blows me away. That far I've gotten and my heart goes out to her, once again.

I guess one reason I am so enthralled is that is what I have had to do for a lifetime. In essence, I was driven to find my sentience.

The worst problem with the prehuman is that it is constantly attempting to justify itself. Economists have celebrated the animal spirt, saying that it is 'natural' to want to do everyone else in for one's own sake. Of course, that is not the wording they use but it is close enough.

I don't know if it's worth it but I thought I would list a few examples of the prehuman reveling in its awfulness.

The current, very obvious example is the exorbitant profits of corporations from inflation that they happily accrue off of the backs of the consumer. In other words, corps jump on the price gouging bandwagon in order to increase profits with little or no regard for those suffering. That is prehuman. That is a prehuman CEO making the bizarre decision that their profits are more important than humanity.

Do you see the broader brushstroke that has been so obvious to me? The misleading direction this gives to some wealthy prehuman thoughts? How people without money are the enemy? And, vice versa, of course. That people with money are the enemy?

Rather than seeing the big picture. The stupour misleads us. Those that revel in making their profits on the suffering of the broader population have lots of confidence but no self-respect. It is the confidence of an animal.

I wonder if the intent of games will change radically? Is the competitive madness just representative of the story told by an idiot? Is it also part of remaining an animal?

Supercharged minds won't come undone.

==========

There is so much nonsense that we believe. You will understand before it disappears from our existence.

My theme song really should be Sade's *Soldier Of Love*.

It's getting annoying. Just when I think I'm done a new crop of insights hit me and no one to share them with on a personal basis.

================

While it seems only a man's problem, it is also a woman's problem. As life progresses, women's conscious awareness kicks in. They realize the imbalance of one-way orgasms.

More than ever, I will say *do not* read the previous books before you have read this one. The previous books just show how difficult it was to arrive at an answer that bypasses all of the deceits, delusions, and confusion that humanity has adopted.

Misogyny.

Men have always considered women subservient. That is the core of misogyny. The reason for that desire to keep women subservient is another matter. I hope you can make the leap. I see no reason to explain it. It is littered throughout my books.

Here is the problem that I have been trying to explain. It covers a lot.

Misogyny has been around for thousands of years. It was spread throughout the male population. It was the expected reaction.

Today, many men intellectually understand that misogyny is a bad thing. That is not enough. It is just like the animal reaction that humanity reverts to at the drop of a hat.

Intellectual understanding is not enough. It is understandable that women pursued this avenue because there was none other to pursue.

More importantly, it was a step along the way to enlightenment.

It has to come from the heart. The heart has to be educated. I don't often parenthesize it but, in all of this, remember, I am not talking about you. I am not talking about me. I am talking, always, in terms of the human race.

=================

deftness, finesse, ingenuity, flair, creativity, agility, adroitness, resourcefulness; underlined by grace, compassion, and love; all reinforced by self-respect and integrity

Self-respect enables self-confidence, self-worth, caring, compassion, empathy, generosity of spirit, honor, integrity, responsibility, grace, joy, decency, honesty, innocence, and the celebration of life in all of its aspects.

=========

noble characteristics, emotional stability, and self-respect

=========

I realize this will mean nothing to the animal that we remain. It is meant only for the human to come.

As I shed all of the convoluted thoughts and see (relatively) clearly, the simplicity of being human strikes me with awe.

The animal has made a complicated, nearly impossible effort, out of portraying the human. Forget emotional balance, self-respect, noble human characteristics. An animal can't even begin to counterfeit those features.

===========

I have this theory about life. Well, I have a lot of theories about life. Like the effect of anaerobic bacteria from the stomach affecting your teeth, gums, *and* hearing as you age. Or, that matsutake mushrooms beat all forms of carcinoma (even if you treat your body and lungs like crap as I did).

I have a lot of them. But, just lately, I've been wondering about another aspect. Telomeres wear out as you age and I began to wonder about the effect of poor nutrition on poor transcriptions throughout the body.

Do our bodies break down simply because we are not feeding it right? I am convinced that it is totally nuts to expect to get all of the necessary nutrition through food alone. I use vitamin cereal, milk, one egg, magnesium pills and a few others in order to *try* to get everything my body needs. But, that happened only after I had begun to seriously age.

How much better would we age if we assured our body all of its necessary nutrition? I can't say I would even give it an outside chance that it would counteract aging but who knows?

I guess the point I'm getting at is that the medical community of the world is all fine and good for dealing with damage done to the body (like broken bones, etc) but I'm not very impressed with much else. The profit motive gets in the way too often (in America) or the acceptance of 'just the way it is' (in England, for instance - it seems like the Rolling Stones song, *Mother's Little Helper*, is right on target. There are a *lot* of pills consumed in England).

All of those behaviours and debilitating situations, of course, will resolve themselves once we become human.

The point I learned while in Asia is that the best approach to keeping the body healthy is *preventive*, not fixing it after the fact.

==============

Why do people have affairs? Because they *know* they are missing something. They *know* there is more to it.

This just shows that our sentience is not in abeyance. It's just that we buried the truth of the matter so deeply that we can't even get at it when the simple truth is right in front of us.

Instead, we veer off into further delusions. We make excuses left and right for having an affair and never ever see the real reason.

===========

I finally understand. I've kept saying that I am done. That 'this is my last book'. Ha! Nope.

The thing is that there is always more to learn. Until prehumanity can get a grip and begin to admit that it is not human yet, I will keep going. There is always more to learn.

Once humanity catches on and begins to accept that it can be human, in other words, once I hear loudly and decisively, I get it; then, I can quit.

Oh, bet on it, I am going to try to quit, once again, tomorrow, when I publish this book. I am at a point where it seems silly to continue to extrapolate but, well, you know.

I don't have any desire to answer all of the questions. First of all, they are endless. Secondly, when you become human, you will realize that it isn't about fame. I am not looking to be famous. Quite the opposite, actually (there's a reason for that).

It is about contributing. I just happen to be in the fuct up position of providing the necessary momentum for humanity to get going. That is the last contribution I can make. If I don't, then the rest of the contribution will be a bit disappointing.

I always did it because there was nothing else truly worth pursuing but, also, it gave me a puzzle on which to work. Of course, then came the lady that her , errr, state, drove me on.

I would dearly love to have contributed this significant step forward for humanity but I have done about all that I can. There are certain things left that I will not do. They begin to fall in the category that I would be betraying my humanity by doing so. I doubt anyone will ever understand that one.

Once it's rolling, once humanity can begin to think for itself, I will be gone. I assure you, you will never hear from whickwithy, again. In this life or any other ... I hate making promises like that. I've broken too many of them not to realize that life *will* throw you a curve. But, I will make it, anyways. It would just be so nice to *begin* living a life as an ordinary human. Not prehuman, they are sad in every way. I have had enough of that. Human.

========

I have often complained about many aspects of authority. Gods, the Milgram experiment regarding authority, the desire to lead and be led. Really, though, as I look closer, it's worse that that and maybe the Milgram experiment really highlights it.

Our sentient ability and interest in thinking is so subordinated that we don't want to think. Even when it could cost someone their lives. On top of that, of course, leaps the animal that drools for blood.

=========

This one probably annoys me the most and I feel there is a hint hidden in the travesty of our approach to goods that can explain a lot about the prehuman state.

========

There have never been truer words than the man saying, "I don't know why she puts up with me/picked me/said yes" etc, etc, etc.

What is truly amazing and must baffle women is that they would never ever mention how lousy a man is at coitus. I've had enough experience with that.

What women don't get is that men are not stupid. No matter whether the woman says a word, the man know. Just note the first paragraph in this dash.

=========

We live by so many myths that only enthrall the prehuman.

Power. It's embarrassing, really. How could anyone grovel at the desire for power.

Gods. As if they ever did anything beneficial for the human race. All they have ever done was nail our feet to the floor.

It is a facade meant to distract us from the truth that we so fear.

=========

We are always looking into our past for answers. There are none to be found there.

We are always looking to our misery for comfort. There is none to be found there.

We must look to the future and celebration, revelry for our humanity. But, we can only do that once we attain our humanity.

This, sometimes I think, is my primary difference from all others. I despise our ancestors. They were never human.

=============

Humanity's polarization is continuing to accelerate because there are no answers in the context of the prehuman. The left and the right both see the holes in each other's arguments but not their own.

That is why I could never join either side of the argument. They are both wrong. Neither has any real answers. It is easy to shoot holes in either side's arguments and both sides know it. They just won't admit it.

It is truly attempting to choose between two deceits. Take your choice. They are both wrong.

You can clamp down on everything or you can let anything go. Neither is an answer. It is avoiding an answer.

People that are desperate to make a name for themselves pick a side and shout at the top of their lungs. It doesn't do anyone any good, including the fool on the hill.

I can't let it go at that. Every time, I try to be even-handed about it but there is a significant imbalance.

The left wing, the liberals are *hoping* for something better. The right wing, the conservatives, are desperately clinging to the past.

What the right wing hates is that the liberals seem to be hopeless dreamers. Without those hopeless dreamers, I would never have been able to make this final breakthrough that makes us human.

I could get a lot more vociferous about what I think of the right wing animals longing to return to the simple ways of the animal, but I won't.

Once we finally gain our humanity and men gain their manhood, finally, the awful remnants of the animal should be permanently gone, including the awful right wingnuts.

The liberals had it right all along, they just didn't know it.

=============

Humanity was never meant to rut like animals. We were meant to love like humans. Because we could never understand this, we created many monsters. Some of them we called gods, some of them were fellow humans.

What makes it so terribly sad is that the actual necessity for the physical expression of love is easy to understand. It is only the awful miasma that humanity created that made it difficult to peer through to the loving act of coitus.

=================

What makes me angry sometimes, the latest stupourdity to fill me with rage, nowadays, is the fact that it wasn't enough for me to discover what has caused humanity to remain as witless as a post, as demented as a presidential candidate, as close to its animal roots that you might as well still be picking your ass with you fingers.

No, I also had to arrange the explanation in a way that could carefully penetrate the eons of stupourdity.

=================

This is the perfect point in history to explain so much of what I have been saying regarding sanity, and the fact that we haven't progressed a smidgeon since we crawled out of our caves tens of thousands of years go.

Depending on which side of the fence you are on, you are pretty certain that the people on the other side of the fence are completely insane. Either you hate all of the change going on or you love it.

You believe in things like vaccines, health care, guns, gods, sex in any way shape or form etc or you don't. The other side is out of its mind.

We tried for the longest time to say that it was just isolated individuals that were insane. That is no longer the case. If you make the pretty easy assumption that both sides are out of their minds, then, that means, that everybody is insane.

Hmmm, this isn't quite progressing the way I wanted. My point is that prehumanity's grasp on reality is insane. The society that we developed is insane for the reason that I have explained in seven books and the fallout from the initial insanity. All along, some people couldn't handle it and they were labeled insane instead of the society that is so very broken but ... frog in hot water. Accept it and everything will be okay. Not so much.

There is the other point, as well. I cannot distinguish between what is going on today and the Nazis of not so long ago, or the Reign of Terror a little further back in history, or the blood-thirsty common folk that would gather round beheading and hangings to vent their frustration and hate on whomever happened to be available to die. Or, the Roman gladiators, or the Persian warriors or the caveman with a club. They all look the same to me.

We put on our finery but the animal keeps peering through.

==========

We are seeing in the world, today, exactly what I have been suggesting. It's not just America. It's not just England. Men's insecurity is in its flaming glory, once again. Their pompous act is nothing more than compensation for their awful failure (that no one will admit!) that has no reason to exist other than inertia. Until they learn how to love, male authoritarianism will always show its ugly face. It will remain until the masses, once again, realize the horror and insanity of it all. Then, once again, it will creep back into the woodwork to blaze, again, in its awfulness at some point in the future. Unless, of course, authoritarianism gains a worldwide grasp, which seems every likely at this stage. Then, we will really be in the cooker. Also, misogyny will never be gone until men no longer hate themselves. It would be so nice if someone finally got what I am saying.

Please do not be stupid enough to point to awful, sick women. If you haven't noticed, those women are under the thumb or 'mentorship' of some awful male.

==========

We have struggled for three millennia to break free from a single lie that the animal left us. Our heightened sentient awareness detected an inconsistency in the animal's way of life. It did not

============

Big History and Little History

Let me just start by saying, read the chapter on Details. There is no reason for this debacle to continue in any way. Women can experience coitus in full measure and men do not have to become moody hulks as they fail.

The more blinders I have pulled off, the more I am *not* surprised that it took us three millennia to figure out what is going on.

The latest, as I pondered my own past, a couple of songs with which I am very familiar, and the Free Love movement, so much became clear.

I began thinking about the first experience of sex for both men and women.

For a woman, she has to go through the pain of losing her hymen or virginity, so it is definitely no thrill for her unless she is incredibly lucky. So, it may take her a few rounds to realize that, while enjoyable, it is seldom the same as it is the man who seems to go into a seizure from a heart attack every single time.

For the man, it is markedly different. He may have already experienced orgasm but what lies ahead for him is an immeasurably extraordinary experience. His brain has one thought during and after the experience. So, it is not a big surprise that it may take him a few rounds to realize that the woman is not experiencing the same extraordinary experience.

As it begins to sink into his brain, it is not big surprise that he becomes moody. What is wrong with him? Why can't he fulfill the woman?

Elsewhere, I go through the later stages of the debacle. How the expectations for love get whittled down to nothing. How men become selfish creatures because they never learn to give in bed in the most magnificent way possible while gazing lovingly into the eyes of their lover.

The point of this is just to show how it messes with everybody's mind right from the start, right on down through history.

Then, there's the big history. How did it play out since we first gained our sentient awareness. I don't have much to go on but I'm guessing it went pretty much like this.

Men will have orgasms due to the necessity of sexual release caused by the buildup of semen. Women can take it or leave it - *unless* they have had the incredible experience.

So, how long did women go along denying themselves the pleasure before they caught on?

It seems the one aspect that became clear very rapidly was that, for a woman, coitus was a bore. The only good for it was making babies.

I say that is clear because there is no other rationale for churches going around shouting sex (of course that means coitus to the churches) is only for making babies! Throw the fear of some nebulous god into them and I'm sure many men walked the line. Of course, back then, there were lots of babies to make, also.

It is clear that pretty long ago, women began catching on to the whole joy of orgasm thing. I just can't pin it down to even a millennia. It really did not become *commonly* accepted that women can have orgasms until less than fifty years ago.

Even today, I have heard women claim they love their man and they don't need no damn orgasm. Of course, these are young women that haven't spent a lifetime fulfilling the selfish desires of their mate.

How many women have gone through life without the most incredible experience of being human and alive?

Male animals are lousy at coitus *from a human perspective*. Men remain lousy at coitus *for no good reason*. Nature made coitus in such a way that a thinking being (that's us) can overcome the limitations of coitus that an animal has to tolerate.

It all comes down to instincts. Animals react with instincts only. Men can think. They can overcome those instincts.

It is easy to do. It is an amazingly complicated story why it has taken us more than three thousand years to realize this.

Half of the human race is driven insane as the reach puberty and attempt to love a woman. The other half is completely bewildered by what is happening.

============

It is the bane that keeps on giving. At first, our poorly mentally equipped ancestors banned any thought on the matter. Next, they created a god to put more emphasis on the ban.

Then, oh then, we began banning anything we didn't like. Just like a witless, demented animal would.

Rather than face the trouble that brought us to our knees, we have confused our very existence, instead.

==================

There is another piece that I have sensed from many women that just breaks my heart. Somehow, because the man cannot last long enough, the woman feels that it is her fault. That she is not attractive enough or who know? Then, just like the man, the problem is compounded because she does not realize it is a common problem for men.

============

The first realization was that coitus was broken for a human, sentient race. Our conscious awareness cannot easily tolerate rutting like an animal. It is not enough. We know it. We cannot avoid knowing it. And, yet, we remained bewildered. We subjugate our conscious awareness because we were not ready to deal with that reality. We must finally comprehend that mankind can easily fulfill the dream of loving coitus for the whole human race, not just the rare, occasional couple - without pills, accessories, or acrobatics.

My growing realization was that loving coitus was the fundamental basis for love in its most glorious form. Without its transformation into a loving human effort, we remain animals. Love begins in the physical form of fully shared pleasure, shared orgasm. That is what has been missing and bewildered humanity for the last three millennia. Coitus, as performed by the animal does not create love. There was no sharing involved. The male takes, the female gives. Men know it better than women. It haunts them for a lifetime. It creeps up on them unexpectedly the first time they attempt to love a woman ... and it all falls apart. It broke our soul long ago. We were left in dismay. We have blocked that realization in every way for more than three millennia because we could never look close enough to realize that it is easy to overcome the witless male animal's failure.

It's not about loving coitus. It is about the fact that we have avoided admitting that loving coitus doesn't exist. We have wallowed in the animal's witlessness for far too long.

We have avoided admitting what our conscious awareness has known all along. Rutting of the animal is not enough for a human. We have never accepted that there can be, must be, more to coitus than the rutting enactment of the animal.

We have run from that conclusion, like scared little children. We accepted, without thought, the failure that had preceded us by a billion years. "That's just the way it is," says the animal.

While loving coitus on its own is important, the deceptions that we have endured, that we put ourselves through regarding its lack, have always crippled any chance at inhabiting a sentient reality, a human condition. We are still acting as prehuman as a Neanderthal in the most important ways.

We have been led far from the realm of reality that suits the sentient state. It is all about the basis for love. Mutual physical satisfaction creates love. It makes love. The giving involved in human, fully shared physical pleasure must be shared equally.

Coitus is the epitome of that goal. We have accepted the meager table scraps of coitus as it was handed down to us by the animal, because coitus is crucial to our existence.

Without coitus, we are extinct. In its current animal form, we remain prehuman, less than the giving, emotionally stable, rational, balanced race of beings we were meant to be.

Do you begin to see the quandary of our ancient ancestors? Coitus was important, crucial. Make any and every excuse necessary but coitus must continue. We are better than that, more knowledgeable, more consciously aware of our state as a sentient race today. It is time to rip off the blinders.

It all became confused, distorted, and meaningfully deceptive. Because we couldn't figure out how to make coitus truly loving.

I have. So, no more worries, if I can get it through your head that we need to learn to love by making love in its most elegant form, coitus. It is easily done. Once we tear off the blinders.

That is the more difficult task. We are inundated with misdirection, outright lies, confusion, and delusion regarding the subject of coitus, as well as our very existence. All because of one lie we told ourselves long ago.

We are already in far better shaper than one hundred years ago when sex, and especially coitus, were strictly unmentionable.

===============

There are just so many that have attacked the problem in some form in the past. I mention Freud and Simone de Beauvoir elsewhere. They attacked it on the sexual front.

One that I find interesting and really, really makes the heart of the problem so glaringly obvious is the Kinsey Report and Masters and Johnson, which are just more recent examples of their predecessor, three thousand years ago, Vatsyayana Mallananaga, who wrote the *Kama Sutra*. In each case, their work was undone by the past.

All of them concluded there is nothing to be done. At least, Mallananaga attempted to provide a solution that worked but, all in all, it has never change. We have accepted that men have a limitation that cannot be overcome.

Spoiler alert: They are all wrong. Read Details below to get to the heart of the problem and become a man instead of a male animal in man's clothing. I hope you get the reference. All of the nightmare tales of our past have a source. Yes, indeed.

But, that is just on the sexual front.

We have been attacking the problem from two fronts, at least, all along. They both converge on loving coitus.

The other front, of course, is love. Jesus, Buddha, maybe the first, most sincere believers in love, made major breakthroughs. So many hat have come since I cannot distinguish from snake oil salesmen. There are a few that come to mind that have sincerely tried, since those two that originally saw the problem, to address humanity's problem from the standpoint of love. At least in my mind, the most powerful of those of late was The Beatles.

My favorite of all is Emerson.

But, it could never be addressed properly until the two converged. That is where the sad, failed attempt of the Flower Power, Free Love, generation really broke things wide open. While all they attained was free sex, they linked the concept of love with the concept of sex indelibly.

===============

One is that now I understand why women turn away from all of this with ease. It has been trained into them from the start. Any woman that dared to broach the subject over the last three thousand years was probably beaten to a pulp eventually. How dare a woman expose men's utter failure? Yeah, that rage of mine at men's ineptitude goes deep.

Here is a totally new facet brought to you by the good offices of a poet I met just a few days ago. In a poem, she wrote (I paraphrase): How stupid of men. They think they know me because they have seen me naked. They don't know me. The actual poem is much better, but that is the point.

This blew open a lot of new facets of our predicament for me. I am still in awe at the insightfulness of the poem and devastated by the heartfelt hurt the poor woman (and, yes, you can essentially make that every woman) feels. They have been put through the wringer since the beginning. It's time to move on.

Do you begin to see why? Let me summarize. No human likes being a failure. The male gender has failed since day one and they take it out on women in every way imaginable. I try to explain this in much more vivid detail throughout all of the books. This is the first and foremost derivative trouble caused by the root cause of our troubles, other than our subjugated conscious awareness. Make no mistake, it haunts men as well as women. This may be hard for a woman to accept because they are the ones that have suffered, but it is the truth. It is disgusting, it lights my rage at the stupour of men, but it is the truth.

As I have said often in the past, men take and women give. It all starts in bed. The poem brought it home to me in a new way.

The poem renewed my spirit to carry on and attempt to explain (my rage at the mistreatment of women has never wavered; just my will to continue to attempt to explain).

It also brought home an amazing finding: that I _try to be_ honest with myself. Don't think that is some high and mighty touting of myself. I kick myself around the block due to my inability to peer into the morass that was made of my mind due to our farcical portrayal of human existence sooner.

===============

As I continue to write and write and write in order to pry everyone's mind's open enough to see what is going on, I keep uncovering new facets, new perspectives, new lenses through which to view the worst debacle of our past and the most glorious event that will define our future.

It is the repetitiveness that drives me crazy. I feel like I should catalogue all of the different (or same) ways in which I have tried to make a particular point.

You know what? Ain't gonna happen. If it is that important, someone else can do it. I suggest cataloguing by topic and the book and page number(s) of the particular assertions. Good luck with that!

=================

Men ruled. Fuck everybody else. That is what our prehuman state amounts to. In some ways, it seems game theory has been working, wearing away at the animal since the beginning. It is beginning to seem a fundamental aspect of nature/existence. Win-win is better.

This last insight seems at the very core of sentience. There will be no love, in its fullest expression, until a win-win situation exists. It is like existence itself insists on an intimate sentient relationship that is built on a foundation of love, equality, and equitable circumstances for sentience to flourish.

===============

As I've mentioned, probably in each of my books on humanity and sex, is that, before I realized that sex (and particularly coitus) was at the heart of why humanity remains so crazy and, finally unraveled the mess of the internal struggle to become human, I had studied other large scale effects, such as laws, religion, institutions, and culture. To put it simply, they are only effects.

What finally now stuns me, because it never crossed my mind before, is the effects of peer pressure. Call it a subcategory of culture. As an overall effect on humanity, it is obviously large. In some ways, it seems like the predecessor to both religions and laws.

Religion was like the formalization of peer pressure. Laws were like its codification.

As I try to look back in time as all of this originated, while simultaneously pondering the current state of the sexual conversation, I have to wonder.

I lived through the powerful transition from the days when sex was just not discussed into the time of "Free Love" (which really always should have been called "Free Sex" since it had so little to do with love) to the current bizarre world which may be best described as "Anything Goes".

All of this shows a powerful movement to break through all of the misdirected peer pressure we have lived with for millennia regarding sex and, in particular, coitus.

The most powerful, disruptive force of peer pressure is always directed at sex and, particularly, coitus.

That has always been the main force behind our inability to talk about coitus, and any other form of sex in any rational manner (I now see how this also blocked my ability to consider and define the problem, even after I recognized it).

It also shows how far back in time it is dated. It existed before the formalization or codification of peer pressure. It is ingrained in us since the day we are born. That is why it has been so difficult to overcome.

It was a natural result of realizing just how messed up we are regarding coitus, while knowing full well that coitus must continue in order for the race to survive. Talk about a rock and a hard place.

We realize that something is missing, after the fact, as we lie in bed and try not to think about it, the pressure begins to build to *never* think about it, which reinforces, after puberty, the strictures that we incur since birth. It engages the second hammer blow to our conscious awareness.

That pressure naturally spawned into the desire to never talk about it, thus peer pressure.

It may be the original source of peer pressure.

As I think about all of this, I wonder if the human that we will become will have any need for peer pressure. Was all of peer pressure inadvertently put in place because we didn't want to talk about how miserably coitus failed? Putting the stamp of the animal on us? Was it a survival mechanism to assure ongoing procreation? Never forget the buildup in any man of pressure for sexual release. Not that anyone will or could.

If you look around at the state of sex today, it is pretty easy to see the vague maunderings that are leading so many to the conclusion that coitus is waste of time. Thus, coitus - and procreation - are being put on the back burner by many.

In other words, we are approaching *another* extinction event in the form of coitus going out of favour. For a rather good reason. We never made it human.

=================

I think everyone can agree that caring is an important component of our existence as a sentient race. I think most anyone would also agree that there is not enough caring going on. It seems likely that most would agree that it is commonly considered a more womanly, feminine trait.

What if we were wrong? What if caring is just as much a male trait that has been held hostage since the beginning by a shadowy force that we have been too bewildered to acknowledge? What if it is a trait that all humanity should carry around with them as intimately as their own skin?

Let's give caring its real, human, sentient name. Let's call it what it is, even though it discombobulates many. The human, sentient term that supersedes all animal expectations of caring is called love.

It is a nebulous word because we have never really come to terms with it. That is because we remain a prehuman animal, so similar to the cavemen that crawled out of the caves millennia ago that it is shocking to admit. The briefcase, the accoutrements, the savvy speech don't make a human.

=====

I look around at all that humanity sets its hopes on and not a single one of them rate with or hold the potential of loving another human fully.

Because I believe that, I feel certain that loving coitus is the only way to fulfill that hope *for humanity*. I italicize because a few finding a way to love in some other way is just not enough. Call it a numbers game, if you like.

Humanity cannot get out of the rut it is stuck in until the vast majority of humanity can learn to love. That requires loving coitus. I'll be blunt. If I had to do it over again, I would jump for joy at the chance to provide cunnilingus in the absence of loving coitus but I do not think it is at all the same. It's certainly better than not. It is certainly better than 'taking care of it oneself', which is how I spent most of this lifetime. But, coitus makes it special. I would be able to look into the eyes of the one that I love during her incredible experience. That is stunningly special.

We obsess about sex because we have never felt fulfilled. That will change when loving coitus becomes standard.

One doesn't need to obsess about sex, once loving coitus has achieved. It provides colour for all of the other activities of being human. It makes everything else in life worth doing. It is more than just act of sex but the fusion of two into one that comes from loving someone completely without any drawbacks.

Does it mean all of the kinks in the systems, cultures, societies, and interactions of humanity transform into a utopian paradise. Far from it. It's just that the dystopia we create is due to the virtual absence of love in its completely fulfilled form. When humanity begins from a place of love, starts from a loving human perspective, everything changes. It becomes stable or, at least, more so.

The reason for the small print is that I wonder still. This woman I adore. I'm not sure I would have met her in another life. Even so, if it had been as late in life as this one, I probably would have hooked up with someone by the time I reached sixty years old.

What I'm trying to get at is what happens to a person when they truly have their wits about them? Don't ask me. I cracked the code on how we get our wits about us but, excuse me, I lived through the same monstrous existence that you did, if you are my age. I'm still quite fuct up. I *know* my thinking is compromised to some extent. I believe very strongly that it would have been radically different if I had been able to love a woman physically the way I always expected was possible - up until puberty.

My guess is that there just won't be ... Let me start, again. We will be coming from a place of love. If I were free at whatever age or time difference I encountered my gypsy queen, you can bet I would have pursued her. Against all odds and obstruction, you can bet I would have pursued her.

But, you see, even there I have to hesitate. In the current situation with this woman that fate has made apparent to me, even in this life, I'm not sure it's not totally insane. So, maybe in a world in which there were not chinks in the armour of my sanity, self-esteem, and noble characteristics, I would know better.

Anyways, what I'm really trying to get at is the situation where a person loves another but, then, runs across someone that knocks them to the floor. First of all, would it even happen? Secondly, let's say it's not just a case of mind-blowing lust, since that seems much less likely to ever happen when one is sexually satisfied with a partner, but something else. Some chemistry between the two that knows no bounds. Would it be pursued?

Honestly, I can't even make a good guess. Could it even really happen? I can't say one way or the other. If so, does the self-esteem make it a non-starter? Again, I can't really say.

I'll give you a suggested reason why none of it would hold up. I don't think we have come close to understanding love. I think love is far more about loving oneself than another. In other words, one can't even understand what it means to love another until one knows how to love themselves. One can't love themselves thoroughly until they know they can do the same for another. I would guess that there may be some women out there that could answer that question validly but it wouldn't be many. It certainly isn't the one that I adore.

If I am right about that. Then the whole suppositional situation would never even exist. There would be no mysterious attraction between two people when one of them was in a stable, fulfilling relationship. Sure, attraction is bound to happen but nothing so off the charts as to disrupt love in its most elegant form.

We have a lot to learn about love, I guess, is what needs to be underlined and bold-typed.

But, I wandered off of the subject of reincarnation. I really want to emphasise how the concept is another part of the puzzle of life that works, even if it doesn't exist.

=========

This may seem unrelated to the words above that, at least to me, are so overwhelmingly profound. Trust me, it is related. This is that which preceded the self-revelations above...

I have slowly been learning that putting a smile on one's face is helpful, but it is not enough on its own.

It was perfect timing. The smile or the mind cracks if the smile is false. My mind has just reached the point that a smile is tentatively accepted. I thoroughly understand why humanity remains a mad animal, even if no one else can follow where I have led. Yes, the last causes the tentativeness. Have I not done enough to explain?

Preceding the revelatory clarity above, I was already feeling liberated. I saw clearly about love, coitus, the animal, the human and the prehuman condition. So, I was feeling pretty good.

I had spent a lifetime in a pensive state beyond anything you can probably imagine. Then, I ran across a smile. That is an understatement in the extreme. Anyways, I decided it was time to adopt a smile. Easier said than done. The muscles involved in a smile, a truly genuine smile, are many. They had not been exercised for many decades.

It does seem to encourage a buoyant spirit but, if the buoyancy is dragged down, it hurts. The smile will feel false, even when it is not.

Then, I realized a smile, alone, is just not enough.

(if all of this doesn't give you a clue as to the state ... well, let me explain in a different way ... I have finally concluded that it is time that I rejoin the human race. It is time to do something that I never had the time, inclination, or luxury to do before. I want to figure you other humans out as individuals. I think that really describes it well. I was overwhelmed by the clamour of humanity so long ago that I dove deep into myself. I never, ever emerged to try to figure out what makes any other individual tick. I was doomed to seek the big picture).

I catalogued the many cockamamie interactions that I either participated in or observed. But, it was just another piece of the puzzle of our mad existence. Why could we no get a gip? It became time, just of late, to start figuring out what makes you individuals tick.

I was just in a store after running around doing a few things leading up to the first serious trip (like airplane and everything) I have taken in a long time. I used to travel a lot (well over a million miles), but haven't done that in more than a decade.

The metaphorical bumps and bruises of preparing for the trip had dispirited me. What provided the juxtaposition, is when I went out to a restaurant the previous night and had the most fun time with a couple that were perfect strangers to me.

All of this was rattling around in my head the next day, while trying to keep a smile on my face (All of the preparations for the trip were making it an effort). I was really not feeling the smile, as I interacted as best I could with folks. The first thing that hit me was how that smile (which was not feeling very real) really put others at ease.

Most important were a couple of interactions that reminded me of just how gracious I used to be (when I was young and not discouraged by the lack of love yet). I now find that it is the distortions of a sentient reality that really hurt all that time.

The smile is nice, the graciousness is crucial. I think either makes it easier, even with an extremely difficult situation.

The graciousness is just so different from the smile. The smile is a matter of muscles and the grace is something else. It is a matter of attitude, but I feel like it is much more than that. I feel like it is a state of inner being, for lack of a better explanation.

It makes the smile work.

Whoa! Whoa! Whoa! It hit me like a ton of bricks this morning. *(now begin to see the connection to the piece above)*

The depths of confusion that our predecessors accepted is altogether mind boggling and, yes, I've been right all along. What drove the lack of reality was purposely (though unintentionally - which is weird) driven by our desire to avoid accepting the reality that coitus is such a mess.

As I pondered smiles, graciousness, and my own past, I realized it is all about the basis of reality. It is all about no longer remaining the vague, distorted reality of Pavlov's Dog. Only by learning love in its physical form, do we become human. Smiles, graciousness, and all of the noble traits that we have tried so hard (and failed) to engender, become natural when we are no longer an animal in human clothing.

This is important because it has taught me to understand and articulate the circumstances in more human, less analytical terms. Just like loving coitus, I can taste the reality of it. *(Now, do you see how this preceded the section above?)*

=======

I'll start with something that surprises me. Again, many dots had to link up to get here.

Technology

I've been considering technology, again (consider it a general consideration that can be expanded like a fractal). And humanity. I have to come to the same conclusion. Some dread technology and think it has ruined us. I have to come to the conclusion that what is wrong with technology is the same that is wrong with everything else regarding our situation (e.g. my thoughts on institutions and surface issues, in general). It is not technology that is the problem. It is the prehumanity that is essentially a demented animal that is the problem.

The perfect example is AI. The perversion of AI is only possible because prehumanity remains perverted.

The idea of AI wiping out humans only makes sense to a demented prehumanity. In fact, an AI would conclude what game theory teaches. Of course, if humanity is stupoured enough to remain prehuman, combative, and denser than a neutron star, then, yes, AI may have no choice.

Once we become human, sane, balanced with stable emotions, the problems go away. That doesn't mean technology will.

A more general instance, we have always been madly (I emphasize the word) driven outward. As I think I wrote in my very first book, we have always been running away from ourselves. That may have been fine (questionable) for the early prehumans. It is not any longer.

What brought all of this to mind (yes, Isaac Asimov) was the thought of space exploration. Once again, we are madly pursuing goals to run away from our problems.

Once we become sane humans, we will still be driven to exploration and new horizons but it won't be a mad pursuit.

In all ways, I am convinced we will be able to ponder the situation in a much more sane manner and move forward in a sane, rational, much more methodical manner.

Our mad pursuits, at this point, are, of course, just getting worse as the vague humanizing influence is drowning in the tandem mad pursuits of profit, toxic masculinity, and national advantage.

The worst problem humanity faces is itself. Once that is resolved, all of our problems become manageable. Easily manageable.

So, yes, I think we will continue to pursue technology. Technology, in and of itself, can be useful - for a human.

I guess it is a straightforward extrapolation but probably still worth mentioning. Gossip and news should go the way of the dinosaur. Gossip almost completely and news in the form of gossip, horror, and outrage; the main staples of today.

Just think about it. News is usually exposing the awful results of remaining prehuman. Like "family gets brutally beaten and thrown to the alligators!" Really, what is the point of even reading that other than to become horrified and share your horror with others? It is like a sick form of glee.

You are not human, yet. It is time to get on with it. We've a long ways to go.

Business. I was just thinking about how big box stores annoy me. The more I thought about it, it wasn't even the big box store concept that annoys me. It is the animal raving desire for obsessive wealth that annoys me. It's not human. There's a LOT of extrapolation that can be done with that. I'll leave it as an exercise for the humans as they arrive on the scene. My guess, is that small quaint shops will make a comeback.

Most everything we have done has been for mad profits. When you really step back and take a look, affordability is not as simple as make it cheap and in mass quantities. I have seen cultures that products may seem expensive and, yet, most everyone can afford them. No, it is not just about driving down the price. All that does is drive up the profits, not particularly improve anything.

I am becoming convinced of what separates me from almost anyone I have ever met.

I am really, really, fucking smart. The *difference* is that I know for certain everyone has the same *potential*. Not just for smarts but for everything that *should* make us human. All we need do is abandon those characteristics that make us prehuman, that come from the animal.

I have started to work on learning to write left-handed. It is very enlightening.

I assure you, it is possible for any human. I expect it will be possible for anyone, once we decide to *be* human instead of acting out the part.

There are a couple of points that makes it so interesting to me. First of all, if I wasn't thinking, it would have been incredibly difficult. I realized, though, that I already *knew* how to write, with my right hand. All I really need to do is *train* the left hand. Of course, there was the added difficulty of learning how to position the left hand for writing. Still working on that.

The second point comes from the first. It is a matter of confidence and that is all, after having learned it long ago for the right hand. If I went into it as impossible, it would have been much more difficult. I probably could have convinced myself it was impossible.

Which brings me to the real point. Men are lousy at sex only because they have been convinced through inertia and silence that they can do no better.

After further review, I am convinced that is not what really separates me from most of the rest of humanity.

No, what really separates me is that I did not follow a single fucking trend.

If you look at all scifi, for instance, they attempt to extrapolate the existing trends. No wonder prehumanity has remained such a disaster.

If you haven't caught on yet, I am in one seriously foul mood today. The dull-witted yammer, the preposterously wealthy gloat as if they have done something special, and the loving get crushed.

I woke up agitated today and it's just progressed. I am so fucking tired of the idiocy of prehumanity. It is infuriating! People read my notes on Post (which I am beginning to suspect is just another ploy by the poor misunderstood lunatics with too much money to manipulate the masses (through AI this time) and give me a thumbs-up.

Funny. I am pretty blunt in any of my comments on Post that it is time to change and that they need to read the previous book. *Not a single fucking one has read the book.* This I know. I even put it for free on Wattpad and *no one* has taken the time to get past the first fucking chapter.

Do you think it is effortless to become human? Do you think I don't have good reason to end my own frustration and leave it to you dimwits to find your own way? (which looks like it's not going to happen, even with my help) Oh, I know, now, how those past folks that were desirous of a loving change had to feel. I am certain they are all spinning in the graves in frustration.

No, I won't go that way. Not on your life. Just as I am not interested in blood and suffering to make it all clear, I am not going to go out of this life feeling defeated. Even if humanity doesn't even begin to get a clue, I will find a way to assure myself that I will not be spinning in my grave. I won't get into that. That's only for my own edification.

I've been pondering beauty, once again. It's weird. It's the human beauty that stands out. While physical beauty of some human beings stands out, we have not been able to differentiate between beautiful features and a beautiful person.

This is mostly true of men. Many men do not distinguish because *they do not care about the person.*

It's is sadly and massively hilarious to me that I have been accused of the same.

I don't know if that catches as it did with me. The animal does not care about anything beyond the physical, that which the eyes perceive.

Do you get it now? Once we are truly human, the person will matter. There is already proof positive because of women that truly know themselves throughout. Those that pass the test of sanity for a human. Those that know that the orgasms must be mutual in order to equate to love.

These women see through to the human. I am not sure there has ever been a male that saw the human without the glitter. It is surely much more rare than women with the same quality of humanity.

===============

Some posts posted on Post before I gave up, once again.

Education of the heart
Or, *The Sentient Struggle For Transformation*

Aristotle said, "Education of the mind without education of the heart is no education at all".

For three thousand years, we have not educated the heart.

Eleanor Roosevelt queried, ""When will our consciences grow so tender that we will act to *prevent* human misery rather than avenge it?"

When we become human. When we educate the heart and accept our sentient state in full.

Unlike intelligence, education of the heart is not a matter of learning from books.

You are about to enter the next level of the game of life. It's called sentience. There's no turning back.

Picking away at each individual problem, like, climate change (as horrible as it is and, yes, it still needs to be addressed), endless wars with no justification, misogyny, inequality and inequitable treatment of so many has done nothing to improve humanity itself. In three thousand years, humanity itself has not changed one iota. Monsters still roam.

Note that all but one of the troubles I mentioned (climate change) have been around *forever* (literally). They are not new. You can legislate until you are blue in the face, and nothing changes until you seek the single source of *all* of these issues. Th real question is what makes humanity so messed up? I guarantee you, the answer will surprise you.

It is not enough to expose our problems. We know what they are. We don't even try to fix them, really. We only try to suppress them. Look around and decide how that's working for us. Attempting to force people (e.g. laws, peer pressure, etc) to act a certain way is infantile. It is an animal's answer to a sentient question. What is wrong with humanity?

The question we have to be asking ourselves is why are we such a dysfunctional race and what do we do about it?

Worst of all, somewhere along the line, we convinced ourselves that we are irreparably damaged. Most everyone believes there is nothing to be done. We are a hopeless cause. Pick away, pick away.

We have only needed to step back and see the big picture. We have to admit that there is something wrong at a very fundamental level.

There is grit in the machine.

The answer, when you look deeply enough, is no, we do not need to remain the horrifying race of inept, supposedly sentient beings that we currently represent.

We need to educate the heart and it is easily done.

=====================

I keep trying to come up with solutions that will fix some aspect of our horrid existence but, until we become human, there are none.

Don't get dispirited. We can be a human, sentient species anytime we decide to do so.

I know how crazy that sounds but it is true. We just have to face reality.

Don't you ever wonder why humanity is so messed up? Believe it or not, it's pretty straightforward.

It took me the longest time to accept what I had found because I was unsure. I couldn't publish for the longest time because of that. I mean, it's kinda big to say, 1)We are not human yet and, 2) it is easy for mankind to gain its humanity, *finally*.

That I took so long to open up, to lay out the situation for others, I think it is a testament to how certain I finally am that this answers all. In some ways, I wish I had waited *another* five years to publish. But, it is so important, and I'm old enough to die at the drop of a hat. I just couldn't wait to explain it as thoroughly, concisely, and decisively, as I can today.

To say I was thorough in my study is ludicrously understated. Seven or eight years before I published the first book, *Sentience* from the time I *knew*. It just seemed unbelievable that it could be that simple. The rest of the books are hashing through three thousand years of nonsense that makes it so difficult for anyone to see the simple, honest truth.

It took all of those years in order to discern the nonsense of a race of beings that, long ago, surpassed its animal limitations but remained bogged down in the stupour of an animal. The stupour is all we have listened to for three thousand years.

Let me tell you, it feels really good to be past so much of the nonsense that we have accepted. I only regret that it took my entire lifetime to do so. Not that it matters that much. It doesn't really mean a thing until all of humanity can cast off the blinders and look up at a sentient reality.

I had researched a *lot* of stuff before realizing what was broken. None of it answered. But, the research was necessary. That was the forty years or so before I finally caught on to what is going on, why all of the lunatic antics continue.

I wrote reams on topics on religions, cultures, and institutions seeking answers. Never published a word of it because none of it answers. Each is just one aspect of the grand nonsense we have endured for millennia. Altogether, they only describe one of the traps.

They just proved to me that forcing the situation is not the way to get there. Our humanity does not come from the outside. Something has been betraying our humanity all along, *from the inside*, affecting the whole human race.

We are naturally human. We are naturally truth-seekers. That's why courts work to the poor extent that they do with prehumanity. We have bungled the truth exceptionally.

I had to search elsewhere. But, I learned the crucial lesson. I don't have a good metaphor to describe the point that forcing morals/actions/behaviours just doesn't work. It doesn't *make* us human. It just makes us *act* human.

As long as our humanity remains an *act*, because it is being forced down the throat by external peer pressure, we remain prehuman. Our humanity needs to flow outward for each individual. It is not book learning, either.

Amidst an existence immersed in illusions and delusions, we remain prehuman. Prehuman is a demented form of animal that still clings to its stupid past never really seeing what sentience means.

What has to be changed about humanity has to come from within. We know what is right. Outside force doesn't make it any clearer. That just forces many down a precarious path of lying to themselves.

We get so caught up in the show that we never even consider that something is fundamentally wrong. Something *inside* the human race needs a sentient adjustment. It is *much* easier to make the change than attempt to explain it.

The actual necessary internal tweak that is required will almost certainly jar you but, once you really, really think about it (if you can), you will not disagree. One aspect of life drags humanity back to the dumbfounded roots of the animal repeatedly throughout a lifetime. The manipulation, the deceit, of humanity has been to hide one single fact of our sentient existence. That led to a sentient animal going insane and never reaching its potential.

You *will* be dumbfounded. The holidays may be the best time to let it sink in.

We can start leading a life as an emotionally balanced, rational, stable, sentient life form any time we decide to do so.

Every time I feel like I'm losing my child-like innocence, once again, it depresses me. I *know* that informed innocence is the only way for humanity. So, I attempt to adopt it. A lifetime of delusions shed is not the same as never having them. So, I do what I can.

Here's the thing. The burden of the mental crap to which we have been exposed, rattles around in the subconscious like a bunch of rocks banging away.

In a little less poetic terms, that missing 90% of the brain that is mourned for its loss? It is just caught up with all of the bullshit we have tolerated for more than three millennia.

It would be nice to just say that all of the bullshit should go away. That is, of course, infantile. We all know it. It's just that the expanse of the problem is massive. It permeates every part of our lives because we never put the animal away. Once you buy into the ludicrous beliefs of the prehuman, you are already all but gone. 90% of your brain becomes consumed by all of the bullshit we accept.

To paraphrase the commercial, "this is your brain on prehuman bullshit. This is your brain without."

If it really is 90% as I think is true, watch out, future humanity! You are about to depart on a wild, fun, enjoyable, ride of challenges that makes sense and revelry as never seen before.

The *human* brain can handle it. A fully sentient, emotionally stable (you do get that is the big change, right?), rational, balanced can handle almost anything (e.g. at this point, our brain wouldn't help a lot if a monstrous asteroid were to smash into us or we don't do something to reverse all of the damage we have caused and that is not just climate change and stupid wars. It is also, for instance, turning the world into a petri dish of violent viruses. Oh, yes, they are all connected. Bet on it.

The trajectory I see, if we don't get our shit together soon, is not good at all.

You need to take a real hard look at what is going on. We go about, doing our best to destroy everything regarding humanity's existence, while we convince ourselves that we are chipping away at all of the offensive behaviour of humanity. That is fine. That is important. It needs to be highlighted how awful we remain in order to do something about it.

But, don't fool yourself, the final answer is not to show, beyond a doubt, how awful humanity can be.

The answer is to figure out what is wrong.

It ends up that it is very much like the thorn in the paw of the lion. It is not a debilitating thorn, as such. Just like the lion, it is an enraging thorn in which many lose their minds.

Education of the heart fulfills every aspect of what is missing in order for humanity to finally become human.

No one seems to be willing to delve deeper into what is wrong. If you take a close look at all of the surface issues of humanity, it comes down to a pretty clear single issue. Prehumanity is plagued by a split personality. Neither version of which has anything to do with a sentient reality.

I like to call it the Practical versus the Dreamer. There are a lot of names for it but those do well. The practical believes that we are nothing more than an animal putting on airs. That is wrong. The Dreamer believes there is more to being human. While that is true, it is misleading because of the way in which we have implemented 'being human'.

What we are really doing is *acting* human. That is not enough. In that case, we are just putting on airs.

Shakespeare was right. *It has been* a tale told by an idiot, full of sound and fury, signifying nothing. We have swallowed, hook, line, and sinker, the idea that it can't ever change.

The problem has been staring us in the face since the beginning. It's just that no one has been willing to look. We all see the problem and flat-out ignore it.

Humanity needs to become integrated with its sentient state instead of running from it.

My poem, *Bifrons*, might apply, though it was written as a self-study.

The split personality must merge and it can only do so by no longer hiding from the truth about the most crucial loving act of being human.

The real question is what causes the split personality. Another clue.

I think I can summarize prehuman life very succinctly: disappointment. That pretty much explains everything. We are so immersed in all of the misery of our prehuman existence that we never look up to see that we can be human.

Why is it that humanity has such a difficult time accepting that coitus is, essentially, lousy in its animal form? Does everyone believe we can do no better? Without pills, accessories, or gymnastics? It's not true.

Worse yet, we have adapted to the situation as an animal would instead of doing what humanity always does: *find a conclusive resolution to the problem.*

That is, loving coitus.

So, women are supposed to be all thrilled about two or three minutes? Really? And, men are supposed to be all proud of lasting two or three minutes?

It's kinda hilarious, really. An animal might be be all happy with that but a human? Really?

We can do better. Uncontrolled ejaculation is for animals.

===============

We don't need people to *act* human. That is what we are doing today. We need everyone to *be* human. We need to educate the heart.

Men have four options in order to be able to act even remotely human. Masturbation, Cunnilingus, Hookers, or Queer (sorry, I think that's an acceptable term). Okay, maybe a dildo will work. It is the best most men can do as long as we accept that we are no more than an animal. It is really stupid.

You have no idea how much it pisses me off that the farthest anyone has gotten through my latest book is one chapter. It seems it is too difficult to think things through.

It's not the shock that comes from Chapter 2 that gets to them. It is the difficulty of working the brain that is required to become human.

Sigh. I really thought I had found a place where people might be willing to think a little. Sadly, it is not true. It is the same people following the herd.

I thought, maybe, it was the limited number of characters on the birdfinger that made people so obtuse, just spouting the same thing that everyone else accepts.

I did not realize how few people there are on this Earth that can think for themselves.

Or, *The Sentient Struggle For Transformation*

I am becoming convinced of what separates me from almost anyone I have ever met.

I am really, really, fucking smart. *That's* not the difference. The *difference* is that I know for certain everyone has the same potential. Not just for smarts but for everything that *should* make us human. All we need do is *become* human. As a species. Not this guy and that girl seeking their navels but the whole human species. It is so much easier than you can possibly imagine.

I am not sure I know how to explain to you what I expect will happen next. Let's see if I can just give a few pointers to lead you there.

1. Ninety percent of our brain!
2. No baggage to drag us down.

3. All of the human qualities on display.
4. All of the wastage, per the prehuman state, gone.
5. Not conflict to speak of.
6. Emotional stability
7. Ninety percent of our brain recovered.

I think that should lead you there. Number seven is not a mistake. It is duplicated for a purpose.

You see the world as a place that everyone struggles for a position. I see a world where everyone is celebrating their existence.

I have to add three last items. They came to me just as I was getting ready to publish the book. I can only hope I can shut up now.

This is, essentially, a rant. It is the reason I feel *fairly* certain I will not be going another book.

I am reduced to ranting in my utter frustration and impatience. I have spent a lifetime observing and never ranting. I hate it. It is prehuman.

If you find something below that helps you understand, great. Just don't expect anything more than a rant. The only reason I am publishing this is because I found a number of the pieces enlightening for me. I hope you do also. Goodness, I hope I am done! Humanity has so much potential, and it is all getting jerked around, right now.

It is very frustrating.

There is an inconsistency in our sentient existence with which we must come to grips. I have done my best to point the way. I have zero concern that I have not elucidated well enough.

The problem is clearly no longer mine. It is a matter of the prehuman excepting reality. I've done all I can. I am *very* uncertain of my success.

Social media. It's right there in the name. *Media.* Right now that disgusts me because media disgusts me. The attempt and desire to induce frothing at the mouth is so apparent.

That does not mean it doesn't have it's place in a sentient world. Media and social media should be the same as the rest of the situation. It is not social media that is the problem. It is the prehumans using it that is the problem. It is the problems that prehumans cause that is the problem, as well as the desire to get people to froth at the mouth.

I am of two minds, though, as to whether social networking will evolve tremendously. I think so. But, I am still concerned that without face-to-face interaction, it can only go so far.

The technology will find a way to assure that meaningful conversations can be accomplished (that is only slightly true today). But, without the physical signals, can it really work? I don't have a clue.

One last try to get across the daunting subject that will change humanity into something human.

I think about my own predicament, which assuredly, in many ways, is far different from most. I cannot think of many that have maintained their sanity that have not become homeless, painful examples of the destruction of remaining prehuman in a sentient existence, and abandoned (repeatedly, which just goes to show how difficult it is) any interaction with his fellow human.

I should clarify. I do not think that anyone that accepts the awful conditions of humanity is sane. That means you and everyone (or nearly) you know.

The ludicrously wealthy and powerful are the worst examples. Do you not see how they play the system for their own gain, at the expense of the rest of humanity? That is prehuman.

The reason I have been forced to reject any interaction with my fellow humans is that I know you are not human. I keep trying to be human but the prehuman baggage goes deep.

Any interaction with the nonsense that all of you accept just worsens the situation. This, I think, may explain the situation better than anything else. How does humanity finally break free from all of the awful derangements that not only have been with us for many millennia but, also, is with us every day of our lives - as long as we deal with others that accept our insane prehuman condition? A guiding light should suffice, if anyone will make the effort.

I hated it. The only thing I hated more was the awful way in which prehumanity treats itself. It is all about the individual. That is an animal construct. For humanity, it is all about the race. It is only tempered by the need for individual preservation. It is not ruled by some mania or other, some obsession or combination of obsessions that are all driven by the individual attempting to convince themselves in some aberrant way that they are human. There is only one change that can accommodate that. It is obviously not currently available to most.

Anyways, where I was really going was that I always felt fraudulent, phony *because* of my failure to be able to love a woman thoroughly. The more I think about it, the more I am convinced that the only men, *under current conditions,* that retain much honesty and self-respect are gay.

It reminds me of a Jackson Browne song. I don't know what it is about writing rhoetry or lyrics but it allows the truth to come out. Even if the truth is not fully recognized by the author. *Pretender* nearly perfectly describes the situation.

I've thought about this a lot and I just don't believe there are many men at all (one in a thousand, million?) that are satisfied with their coital performance. Even if a man can last ten or fifteen minutes, he still must feel - I tried to find a substitute for "out of control" that suited better but couldn't - out of control is the wrong term but it is close. Possibly part of what is missing from the phrase is the feeling of betrayer, liar, and miserable hack - out of control, inept. I learned to avoid women because of this inability to feel 'right' around them. I hated that because I love women. But, what else was I supposed to do? Follow the insane acceptance of the awful unapparent situation like everyone else?

How can a man feel like everything is alright (in a self-directed manner) if he cannot (awww, heck, this is beginning to assure me that I have tried every way to explain this; I'm just repeating) love the one that he so desperately would love to love? The physicality of love has been overlooked because it *doesn't exist for an animal*. Because its potential, its possibility exists, our sentience cannot be satisfied until it is fulfilled.

Then, there is this one that affirms another piece of what I have been saying. Those that have risen to some level of success *due to nothing but circumstances* have to find a way to rationalize it all.

I was reading an online "psychology" article (the quotation marks are supposed to imply what I think of today's definition of human sanity - please see my many comments on the subject, well, all over the place).

The article, to paraphrase, was saying how, "Oh, things aren't that bad and, if you think they are, there is something wrong with you. It is all in your head. Things are definitely getting better." Yeah, right. Until they aren't.

Let me just take a brief survey of how much better things are getting. Can you not see that we are on the brink of our third, and *very definitely* in this case, *World* war? !!! If we avoid it, that will be something.

Do you think it is sane that one country is doing everything it can to destroy another and using its nuclear capability to make sure no one blasts them to smithereens? Do you call that progress?

Do you think the stance that the world accepts *individual humans* leading us to destruction is sane?

Do you think this is the best we can do? Do you think that any government on Earth is so much better than any other that they should claim supremacy? Do you think the push and pull of who can blow up the most is a good way in which to make a final determination?

Misogyny. This one blows my mind. Incel; The Red Pill; the American political party that believes women are lesser beings that require male guidance; religions that *still* believe the same; the growing rebellion against women because they should give sex to any man on his whim because they damn well don't deserve it otherwise? That's improvement??!?! Do you think these are small movements? Do you think things have gotten better for women? Do you think women (at least in America, the shining banner of progress, as well as most countries around the world) can feel safe walking down a dark alley? Do you have any idea how common rape is? Do you realize it goes on in the most respectable households? Well, I getting myself worked up and I have decided not to get worked up ever again. So, off the subject.

Do you think that an intellectual understanding of how awful misogyny, rape, and all of the other collateral damage is enough? Do you think that can ever rid us of the seeds of misogyny?

Geez, I haven't even gotten to the point of talking about climate. We are on the brink (actually I am rather convinced we are *beyond the brink*) of the worst destruction ever recorded because *the human race* cannot decide that it is on the brink of destroying the climate, all because a lot of people are making big bucks off of fossil fuels!!

Enough! I could go on for days regarding all of the awfulness that the human race currently represents. This is the problem I face. I have said all there is to say and I am reduced to ranting. I *do not* rant!

I avoided getting worked up about it for a lifetime. All of the feeble efforts to right the surface issues are token efforts of a demented animal that cannot see its way past its animal legacy and embrace its humanity, its sentience.

Enough.

Thank you for reading this. I hope someone gets it. I hope one of the previous books makes it so. I have done everything possible to make sure that this is not the first book someone picks up.

whickwithy@gmail.com

www.ingramcontent.com/pod-product-compliance
Lightning Source LLC
Chambersburg PA
CBHW071058280326
41928CB00050B/2554